GOD'S INCREDIBLE PLAN

God's Incredible Plan

Martha McCallum and Jane Hamblin

Fleming H. Revell Company
Old Tappan, New Jersey

Library of Congress Cataloging in Publication Data

McCallum, Martha.
    God's incredible plan.

    1. Providence and government of God—Biblical teaching. I. Hamblin, Jane, joint author. II. Title.
BS544.M33   231'.5   78-621
ISBN 0-8007-0905-5

Contents

Foreword

If you have ever said or heard someone say, "The Bible is so difficult to understand," you will really appreciate the purpose of this book. We all have memories of unrelated Bible stories; David and Goliath, mighty Samson, Noah and his ark, Jonah and the whale. But it is impossible to understand any related significance of these stories if they are merely viewed as an unrelated collection of bits and pieces of literature, heroic dramas, philosophy, history, and wise sayings.

My personal belief is that most of the criticism that the Bible receives as not being accurate comes from taking one verse or portion out of its larger context and failing to see that there is a fantastic unity which ties it all together. Most people study the Bible in about the same way they would put together a jigsaw puzzle. They find interesting pieces that seem to hold promise of larger assemblings but no sensible picture emerges until all the pieces have fallen into place. Then you can see the value that each separate piece played.

This same thing is true of the Bible. There is an Incredible Plan that runs throughout the whole Bible from the first Book of Genesis to the last Book of Revelation. Not only does it give a sensible picture of the workings of God in the lives of men of ages past but this plan also gives promise of God's continued intervention in our personal lives in the twentieth century and in the affairs of nations.

Martha McCallum and Jane Hamblin have been teaching these liberating truths to the churched and the nonchurched for years with incredible success. I, for one, am thrilled that they have finally put this in print so that countless thousands more will be given the opportunity to understand the great plan of God for His creation and for their personal lives.

HAL LINDSEY

Preface

When our publishers suggested writing a preface, we had to admit we didn't know what to put in a preface. After some consideration, we have concluded there are some things we would like you to know about this book. For one thing, it was not "written" but rather it took form during a pilgrimage—a journey of *learning to know God's Word* and then of really *knowing God.* Finally, our pilgrimage was one of *learning to communicate God and His Life* to other people—both in and outside of church life.

Many people encouraged us to write this book. Most told us they were surprised to discover the one, simple story continuously revealed in the Bible even though it was written over hundreds of years. Many of these friends have told us the main cause of their former unbelief and disinterest in "religion" was ignorance. This lack of understanding of the Bible caused them to have a small and inadequate idea of God, instead of knowing what God and His plan are really like.

Our objective in this book is to present God as real and His plan for Planet Earth as understandable as it is incredible. Our hope through this simple presentation is to turn the reader's mind and heart toward the **Objective Reality,** which is God, and to encourage the reader to walk forward with God as an active participant in His Incredible Plan.

In conceiving and writing this book, we have been influenced and inspired by many godly men and women. We would especially like to mention Mrs. Alta Hoyt, Mr. Hal Lindsey, and Mr. Bill Counts. We are particularly indebted to Bill and Hal for the material in chapter 12. For the reading and correcting of our manuscript, we thank members of our families and fellow members of our larger family, the Body of Christ. Special thanks goes to Ann Blackwell for her patient typing and retyping of our manuscript. And we express our deep appreciation to Dr. Roger

Blackwell and Dr. Wayne Talarzyk for making it all possible. For the many hours of editing and rewriting, we are deeply indebted to Roger Blackwell. Without his expertise, this book never would have been published.

We want you to know that we make no claim to a high level of biblical scholarship. Our purpose and theme is to present simply the reality of God and the reasonableness of His plan in our universe. It is our desire that you also will know His Presence and Power in your life.

MARTHA MC CALLUM
JANE HAMBLIN

GOD'S INCREDIBLE PLAN

1
God Is

Most people are overwhelmed on a clear summer night as they look up at millions of twinkling stars. On such a night several thoughts come to our minds at once. Perhaps the first thought is of time or distance, that the light of the nearest star has reached us after travelling at the mind-boggling speed of 186,000 miles a second! The next thought which our minds grapple with is the immensity of the universe—our imaginations try vainly to cope with the concept of infinity. Then we may think of the age of our universe. Many scientists consider it four billion years old, a span of time beyond our comprehension. Compared to the age of our universe and its size, the length of our lives shrinks to almost nothing. Someone has said the history of man on Planet Earth is like one second in the twenty-four-hour day of the earth's life. In contrast, how insignificant our own seventy-odd years of life seem to be!

Is There a Purpose?

People are asking searching questions in our technological age. Is there a purpose to it all? Does it matter that we are here? Why is there a universe rather than nothing at all?

Those who are humanists or naturalists would answer no to the first two questions. They would say there is no overall purpose to the universe and no uniqueness in man himself. Their answer to why there is a universe at all would be to say the question is absurd. But is it absurd? Humanism, by its very definition, has no absolutes and provides no answers to the deepest questions about our lives. All its answers are necessarily limited to those which man himself has or can find. The British philosopher-math-

ematician Bertrand Russell, speaking from the naturalist viewpoint, is a good example. He views man as the "accidental collo-
cations [ordering] of atoms" and all of our labor and our genius
are "destined to extinction in the vast death of the solar system,
and that the whole temple of Man's achievement must inevitably
be buried beneath the debris of a universe in ruins" (from *The
Basic Writings of Bertrand Russell,* edited by Robert E. Egner
and Lester E. Denonn).

As humans we rebel against the idea that we are insignificant.
We do not easily think of ourselves as some sort of humorless
joke or a mere accident. Nor do we feel the universe is without
reason or cause. And rightfully so; there are valid reasons that lie
behind our feelings. God's Incredible Plan is written from this
belief that there *is* a purpose to the universe, that we can know
what it is, and even more importantly, that we can be a significant
participant in God's plan.

It is written on the premise that God does exist and that He has
communicated with us. The logical and scientific proofs for God's
existence are elaborated in Appendix A at the end of this book.

God's Point of View

As human beings we are limited by our time-and-space physical
existence. We are the participants in the "parade of life" through
the separate moments of time which we experience. On this plane
it is our privilege to enjoy God's creation and have meaningful
human relationships during our life span.

An even greater privilege is open to us, however, since God has
made it possible for us to rise above the plane of time and "see"
from His point of view. It is rather like viewing the "parade of
life" from a helicopter which is in eternity or "outside of
time."

Our vision is enlarged and our moment of time expanded to
include God's larger overall plan for His creation. God created us
to live life fully here on Planet Earth and yet be anchored by His
eternal perspective. Because God loves us He wants us to understand His plan and how we can fit into that plan in our own unique
way.

This book is our simple presentation of God's Incredible Plan from His point of view. "Seeing" His plan is only one step from "believing" and becoming a part of it.

It is our hope that all of you who read this book will participate in both "seeing" and "believing." As the Apostle Paul prayed, "May the eyes of your hearts be opened so that you can see something of the future He has called you to share and the riches He has for you" (*see* Ephesians 1:18, 19).

2
Behind Time

Since God is there, it is absurd to think He would leave us, His created beings, to stumble through history without any revelation about Himself and our relationship with Him. It is equally absurd to suppose that His revelation would be anything less than perfect, complete, and clearly presented. This He has done in time and space. We are calling this revelation God's Incredible Plan. God has a plan to satisfy man's needs, his deepest longings, and so answer his questions.

To understand God's plan for Planet Earth, it is necessary to start at the beginning or even, in a sense, before the beginning. Regardless of how difficult you and I may find the concept, there was existence before time or outside of time. That existence is called eternity. To understand the nature of eternity and eventually the nature of our own universe, we must begin in that shadowy veiled portion of God's plan long before the universe was brought into existence. We must try to understand events that take us behind time itself.

God has revealed numerous essential elements of His plan as it unfolded behind time even though He has not chosen to reveal to us all the details of these events. At several points throughout the Bible, however, He provides insights about those events with enough detail to allow us to know the nature of eternity, why time began and how it will end, and the meaning of the great conflict which we observe in the universe.

The Creation of Angels

Before time began, God created an order of beings called angels. This creation of angels was before man or the universe was brought into existence (*see* Job 38:7). In the minds of many people, angels have been confined to roles singing Alleluia in Christmas pageants. Now it appears that the topic of angels is becoming of more widespread interest and study. (Examples of this interest include Hal Lindsey's *Satan Is Alive & Well on Planet Earth* and Billy Graham's book *Angels: God's Secret Agents*.)

Angels are exceedingly numerous, according to the Bible. They were not born but were all created at the same time (*see* Daniel 7:10). They are mighty and powerful, having supernatural strength (*see* Psalms 103:20). They are not mortal and have complete mobility in that they can move from place to place in an instant.

Angels were created in the image of God as spiritual beings and because of that, they have a will or self-determination. They also have intellect, emotion, and eternity of existence.

The will of each of the angels was in perfect harmony with the will of God in eternity. The quality of eternity is one will, namely, God's will, as Donald Grey Barnhouse points out in *The Invisible War*. The quality of time, conversely, is the existence of more than one will. As long as God's will was perfectly accepted, events occurred outside of time, or "behind time." Time began when another will, described later, came into existence. It is

somewhat ahead of our story, but we can also conclude that time will end when God has finally placed all things in order once more. Then eternity will begin again with His created beings who choose to do His will.

These paragraphs are illustrated in Figure 1 which shows **Eternity Past,** that period of non-time that existed before the creation of the universe and time-space realities which we know on Planet Earth. Figure 1 also shows that time will cease to exist at some point and we will enter into a new period of non-time, like **Eternity Past,** which will be called **Eternity Future.**

The Angelic Rebellion

Sometime after these angelic beings were created—perhaps eons—the highest and most honored of all angelic creation rebelled against God and in so doing, introduced the principle of unrighteousness (sin) into the universe. More simply stated, this highest and most honored being chose self-will in place of submitting to God's will. This event describes sin and helps us to understand that at the root of every sin is the element of exalting created will over God's will.

Lucifer the Beautiful. There are two good reasons for understanding more about Lucifer, the angel who led the rebellion against God's will. First, we must understand the nature of Lucifer and his activities if we are truly to understand current and historical events on Planet Earth. Second, there are many misconceptions about Lucifer which portray him as some type of unattractive, bumbling, medieval character rather than revealing his true nature.

In one of those rare glances provided by the Bible into **Eternity Past,** Lucifer is revealed as next to God Himself; he was the "anointed cherub" (*see* Ezekiel 28:11–17; Isaiah 14:12–14). He was not only the highest and most honored but also the wisest of all angelic creation. God said to Lucifer, "You were blameless in your ways, from the day you were created until unrighteousness was found in you" (*see* Ezekiel 28:15). The unrighteousness that was found in Lucifer was that he set his will against the known will of God. Lucifer said, "I will raise my throne above the stars of God . . . I will make myself like the Most High" (*see* Isaiah 14:13, 14).

Into a perfect environment, unrighteousness (sin) entered with the choosing of self-will over God's will. Lucifer had the ability to choose his own actions (self-will) and he chose to reject the plan or will of his Creator. In so doing, Lucifer deliberately disobeyed the first law of created beings—*that the created should submit to the Creator*. Instead, Lucifer chose self-deification and became the adversary of God.

Lucifer's Mirror Kingdom. Lucifer's rebellion was far more significant than the act of just one angel. This is true for three reasons. First, the rebellion was significant because of Lucifer's abilities or position as the highest angel, second only to God Himself. Second, he took a third of the angels with him. These angels are known as demons or fallen angels throughout the Bible (*see* Revelation 12:3, 4, 7).

The third and most significant reason was Lucifer's desire to make himself "like the Most High." He wanted to be worshiped as god. He set up his kingdom as a counterfeit of God's Kingdom on Planet Earth. The nature of this "mirror kingdom" is portrayed in Figure 2.

The lower portion of Figure 2 displays the counterfeit world system which appears real. The upper portion depicts God's Kingdom of lasting reality. It requires discernment to determine the difference.

Lucifer, Master of Deception. Lucifer—or Satan as he is now called (a name which means "adversary")—rules the kingdoms of this world for "the whole world lies in the power of the evil one" (*see* 1 John 5:19). In addition, he gives power or authority in his kingdom to whomever he pleases in return for worship of himself (*see* Luke 4:6–7). He is a master of deception, presenting his kingdom as the most attractive, self-fulfilling alternative available. Because of this, Satan is called "the god of this evil world" (2 Corinthians 4:4 LB), "an angel of light" (2 Corinthians 11:14 LB), and "servants of righteousness" (2 Corinthians 11:15).

Satan is not a hideous little man with horns, running around in red flannel underwear, as he is often portrayed by those who do not take him seriously. Instead he is the master of deception and confronts people in most attractive and appealing ways. As stated before, it requires real discernment to be aware of the devious ways in which Satan seduces us into following him, which eventually results in our worshiping him.

Why Not Now?

The question that comes to mind for many people is, Why does God allow this mirror kingdom of Satan's to exist? Why doesn't God put a stop to this deception? God is allowing Satan's overall kingdom to reach completion because God has made it clear that if a will is set against His, the result will be chaos, anarchy, and death. For a while, God allows both kingdoms—His and Satan's—to exist side by side on this earth. During the period we know as **Time,** all created beings will eventually see this eternal truth verified. What looks so "good" and so "real," proves to be the very source of evil and unreality and will face final destruction. Although Satan is allowed to operate for a time, that time is only an instant when compared to eternity.

The rebellion of Lucifer does not go unpunished. Lucifer has set up his kingdom, counterfeiting God's Kingdom, but God has already judged and sentenced Lucifer, or Satan as he is now called, and all of the rebellious angels. The execution of that judgment is pending while events on Planet Earth are unfolding. That judgment *will* take place at the end of time, just before **Eternity Future** (*see* Matthew 25:41).

Review

To review this chapter, we see the sequence of events behind time in God's Incredible Plan: the sequence of God's perfect creation, rebellion by Lucifer and his followers, judgment of the rebellion, and the beginning time and space on Planet Earth, from God's point of view.

On this same earth the focal point is a very special piece of real estate. (It is in the Middle East, which is to become the cradle of civilization and where the stage is set for the next creative act of God: mankind. It is also the stage for the continuing drama to follow.)

God elected to create another order of beings as a demonstration of His Love, Justice, and Wisdom. The angels will be taught many lessons about His grace and His forgiveness as they observe the journey of man through time.

3

History Begins

The stage is set for the unfolding drama in the conflict between God and Satan. The stage is a special piece of real estate on Planet Earth, known today as the Middle East. God's Incredible Plan will inexorably be played out and every individual will have the opportunity to be a part of the plan. (It is the nature of God's universe that both of these concepts remain true: God's Sovereign Plan versus man's free choice. *See* Roger T. Forster and V. Paul Marston's *God's Strategy in Human History* and Clark Pinnock's *Grace Unlimited*.) The participants will have the free choice to accept the roles provided by God for them in His plan or to resist and reject them. There are only two kingdoms on Planet Earth: God's Kingdom and Satan's kingdom, hereafter called *the world system*. And man was created to be a participant in this conflict.

God Creates People

In the first chapter of the Bible (*see* Genesis 1:27), God tells us that He created man in His own image. This means that people are like God in His faculties, having a will, emotions, a mind, and eternity of existence. God called the man He created *Adam*.

Man Has a Three-Part Nature. God created man with a three-part nature. The three parts of every person are: body, soul, and spirit (*see* 1 Thessalonians 5:23). These components are illustrated on page 24.

Body. The outer circle stands for the outward man or the material body. The body is the instrument used for the expression of the soul to relate to the world around him, using the five senses of sight, smell, hearing, taste, and touch. The Bible states that the body is composed of the basic elements ("dust from the ground") of the earth (Genesis 2:7).

Soul. The second part of a person is soul. It is the part of us that

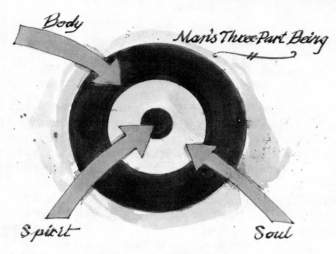

is our personality. Soul includes mind, will, emotions, moral consciousness, and eternity of existence. The mind is that part of our personality that has the capacity to understand God's character, to interact, to have rational thought, and to have memory. The will refers to the ability God gave us to choose and with it there is the enormous risk of choosing against God. There is also the privilege of choosing for Him. Emotions encompass a person's ability to respond emotionally and personally to God and to his fellow men. Moral consciousness and awareness of eternity of existence set man apart from the animal kingdom and it is with these faculties that man realizes God exists and that he himself will exist beyond death.

Spirit. Central to the basic nature of every person is the most incredible dimension of all, the spirit. With the creation of man's spirit, God "breathed into him the breath of life" (*see* Genesis 2:7). In giving man a spirit, God gave him the capability of receiving the very life of God which is Eternal Life.

Free Will, God's Will, and Self-Will

God desires to have a love relationship with us, His created beings. Only a free being with an independent will can love because love requires freedom of response in order to be meaningful. In other words, in order to love, a person must have the choice not to love. Free will, however, introduces the genuine possibility of the wrong decision—the decision to reject or not respond to God's will. When the created person sets his own will against God's will, it is sin or self-will which results in chaos, anarchy, and eternal death.

Purpose of Man's Creation. To understand the purpose of man, it is essential to realize there are four levels of life in the universe. These levels are: divine Life (the highest) which is God's Eternal Life, angelic life (second highest), human life, and finally, animal and vegetable life (*see* Psalms 8:4–6).

Man is created like a glove, to contain the very highest level of divine Life, which is Eternal Life. To carry the analogy further, an empty glove is flat. Although the glove is shaped like a hand, it cannot function in the capacity for which it was intended until a hand is placed in it. So it is with man until he contains God's Eternal Life.

It is part of God's amazing strategy to create man and commission him to subdue and to rule over all the earth. The only way man could execute this responsibility, and thus fulfill his purpose, is to contain God's divine Life. Without God's divine Life man is ruled by angelic life, namely, Satan and his world system.

In addition to this purpose for man, God desires to have a vast family of people who will function as His vice-regents, expressing His very Life. It is incredible that the God of the universe has invited us to be His "revealers" or the "manifesters" of His Kingdom on Planet Earth.

Two Significant Trees. In the middle of God's Kingdom (the Garden of Eden), two significant trees were placed. There was the "tree of the knowledge of good and evil" (Genesis 2:17). God told Adam that the day he ate of it, he would die. The other significant tree was the Tree of Life. It depicted Eternal Life and Jesus Christ is spiritually the Eternal Tree of Life (*see* Revelation 22:2).

Adam had the choice of whether or not to eat of the tree of knowledge of good and evil. Because he chose to disobey God, he made it impossible to eat of the Tree of Life. Had he eaten of the

Tree of Life, he would have contained the highest life, divine Eternal Life, which is the Life of Christ.

God's Kingdom Invaded.   Satan, the enemy of God, is described in the Bible as "roaming to and fro on earth" (*see* Job 1:7). He is pictured as shrewd and as one who prowls around like a lion seeking someone to devour (*see* 1 Peter 5:8). His basic strategy is revealed as accusing God to man (*see* Job 1:11 and Genesis 3:5) and accusing man to God (*see* Revelation 12:10). He is determined to thwart God's plan and by causing additional rebellion against God, to build up his own kingdom.

In the Garden of Eden, Satan's attack against God was to cast doubt on His Word and the goodness of God and to convince Eve that by challenging Him, she would be like God (*see* Genesis 3:5). Satan's plan was to convince Eve that God was trying to suppress her, keeping her from being fulfilled and knowing as much as God. Satan made his temptation of Eve a moral issue; it resulted in belittling God and deifying man. In believing the lie, Adam and Eve chose death, and lost the opportunity to eat of the Tree of Eternal Life.

There is a tendency to think the choice was between good and evil. It was not. The choice was Eternal Life or eternal death. The forbidden tree was the knowledge of *good* as well as evil. Eating it resulted in death whether Adam and Eve did good things or evil things. Choosing this tree represents human life without the Life of God and that may be very good or very evil but it always ends in eternal death.

Man died, back there in the Garden of Eden, just as God had said: "The day that you eat of it you will die." Man's spirit, the part of him which was to contain God's Eternal Life, died that day. That is, man's spirit became atrophied or dead since it was no longer capable of understanding and experiencing things of the spirit (*see* 1 Corinthians 2:14). As a consequence, the soul became the controlling part of man separated from God. Furthermore, the body of man became "perishable" (1 Corinthians 15:53), meaning that man would experience physical death. This very real event in history was the Fall of Man from personal fellowship with his Creator.

Once man had made his choice, separation from God took place. This separation included expulsion from God's Kingdom into the world system. After God expelled Adam and Eve from His Kingdom, He placed an angelic being with a flaming sword to guard the Tree of Life. It was not possible for Adam and Eve to eat of the "tree of death" and at the same time eat of the Tree of Life.

God's Problem: Man

God had a problem when Adam and Eve chose against Him. To understand this problem, it is necessary to examine the character of God and His attributes. A picture of God and His attributes is shown in Figure 3.

God's Attributes. There are some things that God cannot do. For one thing, God cannot lie. The reason He cannot lie is that he is **Veracity,** the very source of truth.

God is a **Just** God and is the **Sovereign** of the universe. He is also **Immutable** or unchangeable. As God, He cannot express one of His attributes at the expense of another one. Therefore, He cannot express **Love** at the expense of another attribute such as **Justice.** Since Adam and Eve challenged His will and set their lives against Him, God had to deal with that challenge justly. The problem facing God was how to deal with Adam and Eve with both **Justice** and **Love. Separation requires reconciliation.** Reconciliation means the bringing together of alienated parties by solving the enmity between them. God is the One who **Loves** His created beings and yet at the same time, He is the One who must **Justly** judge their rebellion against His **Sovereign** right to rule. Being **Immutable** (unchangeable) and the source of **Veracity** (truth), He must carry out His sentence of death (eternal separation). The heart of man's sin is self-will but a **Righteous** and holy God cannot allow sin in His presence. By God's **Omniscience** (all-knowledge) and **Omnipotence** (almighty power), He *progressively reveals* to man down through the ages the Redemptive Plan which will crush and defeat Satan, as well as reconciling man to Himself. Man's condition, simply stated, is that we do what we do because we are what we are!

God's Solution: Redemption. God's plan for reconciliation, which must be based on both **Love** and **Justice,** is His Redemptive Plan. Redemption simply means buying out of slavery by paying the ransom price. This plan is also the greatest revelation of God's Wisdom and Power in all of history. Even in Eden, God gave the first picture and prophecy of His solution when He said to Eve, "From the seed of the woman will come One who will crush the head of the serpent" (*see* Genesis 3:15). This was a promise of the eventual defeat of Satan at the hand of One who would be born without a human father. This was the first prophecy of Christ's coming to earth born of a virgin, and of the work He was coming to do (*see* Galatians 4:4).

Christ's coming and God's plan of redemption is visually described in Figure 4 as the great River of Truth. This first revelation in the Garden of Eden is expanded and amplified throughout the Bible as God reveals His solution for man's condition.

Two Significant Sacrifices

The story of man continues, revealing the significant differences in his religious approach to God. These differences are illustrated in the two sacrifices offered by Adam's sons, Cain and Abel. The two sons were outside of God's Kingdom, the Garden of Eden, and living in the world system run by Satan. This was a result of man's rebellion and we shall now see how sin progresses and bears fruit. Adam's original sin was against God but we shall see that Cain sinned not only against God but also against his brother, illustrating the natural progression of sin.

Cain's Religion and Abel's Relationship. The two brothers, Cain and Abel, each offered sacrifices to God. Cain brought the "fruit of the ground" (Genesis 4:3) as his offering and God did not accept it. Abel, on the other hand, brought by faith the sacrifice of an unblemished animal which God accepted (*see* Hebrews 11:4). Why was one rejected and the other accepted?

God was not playing favorites with Cain and Abel. Both were Adam's sons and were as fallen and alienated from God as was Adam. Both brothers were equally religious in the sense that they

each brought offerings to God. The difference, however, was in their heart attitudes.

Abel's sacrifice. Abel offered his sacrifice according to God's requirements. He responded to God by faith and, because of his obedience, God accepted Abel's offering. His sacrifice was important because it revealed something of God's Redemptive Plan, even though Abel knew little of its future significance.

Abel's sacrifice was a "copy of heavenly things to come" (*see* Hebrews 9:23) or another tributary to God's River of Truth (*see* Figure 4). Abel offered up an unblemished animal which God had designated as a picture of what He was going to do about man's problem of sin (*see* Leviticus 17:11). This principle of the death of an innocent and blameless life substituting for the guilty one is used throughout the Old Testament. The only way that a sinful man can live with God forever is for a sinless life to die in his place. Here we have a preview of God's Redemptive Plan in embryonic form. An expanding revelation of the details will unfold in the years to come.

Cain's sacrifice. Cain's sacrifice was brought as a religious exercise rather than an act of faith. There are two ways people attempt to approach God. One is by faith, as Abel did, bowing to God and responding to His Word. The other way is by saying, in effect, "God, bless my plan, bless what *I* am doing in Your name," without a sense of sin and recognizing no need of God's forgiveness. God alone can see a person's heart and judge whether the person is responding in faith or functioning self-sufficiently. The contrast between a relationship by faith and a religious self-effort continues through all the history of man.

Cain's Escapism. When God exposed Cain's heart, he killed his brother and in so doing became the first murderer. Faced with his sin, Cain tried to escape God's question about Abel by arrogantly responding, "Am I my brother's keeper?" (Genesis 4:9). The response of an unbelieving heart is often to parry any question which exposes its utter sinfulness. God's Light is so penetrating that each one of us will either respond and bow to Him or attempt to escape from Him so that our evil deeds will not be brought to His Light (*see* John 3:20, 21). We have all thrown up smoke

screens or tried to change the subject when God's Light exposes
our sin. A contemporary version is, ''What about those who have
never heard God's Word? What about the heathen?''

Kosmos—the cult of man. Cain escaped or went out from the
presence of the Lord and established the cult of man, the Kosmos, a system which *appears* to prosper and continue without
God. Man in rebellion against God erects a system, or a wall
around himself, which is his own substitute for the God he wants
to ignore. In man's system, God's personal involvement is locked
out, resulting in the deification of man and his accomplishments.
Man builds his own relative moral system without reference to
God's Absolutes. It follows that man's moral system is always
lower than God's because of its reliance upon relative values
rather than God's absolute morals.

Seth Starts a New Line of Men.   Another son was born to Adam
who was named Seth. He started a new line of men who began to
build personal relationships with the Lord: they knew the Lord
and walked with Him willingly.

Noah's Walk

Hundreds of years later, as man progressed through time, rebellion against God increased and became full blown. It would
seem that God's Kingdom was waning and headed for failure.
Even God Himself was grieved over the hopeless condition of
most of His created beings. The Lord saw ''that the thoughts and
imaginations of man were evil continually'' (*see* Genesis 6:5). He
is not, as some picture Him, a stoic: He sees, He is involved, and
in this instance, He is sad.

God's Safe Refuge.   God, the Creator of the heavens and the
earth, is never caught unawares. His Kingdom will never end. No
matter how hopeless the earth's condition and man's rebellion
may become, God always continues His plan and does so with a
willing man. Here God's man was Noah who, with his family,
walked faithfully with Him. As God prepared the first full-scale
judgment of the rebellious, unbelieving world system, He ordered
Noah to build the ark as a refuge for his family, who were the only

remaining followers of God. The ark is a symbol of God's complete Provision for His followers' safety and security. Noah and his family willingly walked into the ark and God Himself shut the door of the ark for the duration of His judgment.

A Demonstration of God's Character.   The Flood demonstrates God's character. His Holiness and Righteousness are expressed as He judges man, who has completely corrupted himself and violated Planet Earth. It is a dramatic demonstration of God's Holy Wrath, His Justice, and His Power (Omnipotence). It also demonstrates His Love as He saves those who respond to Him.

It would seem that man would learn from this demonstration of the consequences of rebellion. Unfortunately, this is not true and Jesus warns that the same level of corruption that prevailed before the Flood will be repeated at the end of man's history. Until then, however, God continues to deal with us patiently for He does not *want* anyone to perish (*see* 2 Peter 3:9).

A New Beginning.   When the earth had sufficiently dried, Noah and His family emerged from the ark, and with that event, the human race had a new beginning. After demonstrating His judgment of sin and rebellion and His preservation of His followers, God also entered into an unconditional covenant with Noah, promising that the earth would not again be destroyed by a flood. The rainbow was given as a sign of this promise by God.

4

Nations Divided—A Nation United

A historical link between Noah and Abraham is provided in Genesis 10 and 11 in the Bible. The events in this era demonstrate how subtle the revolt against God can be. This period in God's revelation is so important that special emphasis is needed.

The System: The Way of Man

Nimrod's Tower of Idolatry. Nimrod was a mighty king who built six of the ancient cities of the world. Two of those cities were Nineveh and Babel, later to be known as Babylon. His ambition was to make *himself* a name and to establish a world empire. To accomplish this, Nimrod led the people in building a huge temple-tower, which was to be "a proud, eternal monument to themselves" (Genesis 11:3, 4 LB).

The tower in Babel was apparently an astrological observatory like the ziggurats which remain today in that part of the world. Astrology is the worship, not of God, but of the sun, moon, and stars. Romans 1 tells us that if a person does not worship God the Creator, his first step away from God will be worship of the creation.

The people started to build the Tower of Babel. Their motive in building the tower was "to reach God," meaning to attain the position of God. Nimrod's more specific motive was to keep mankind together under his own leadership. When the Lord observed these events, He said, "Look! One people, and all with one language [purpose]! The way they are starting to behave, nothing they plan to do will be impossible for them" (Genesis 11:6 MLB). This is God's view of an indisputable historic fact: Fallen men without barriers greatly accelerate the rate of rebellion.

The bricks of Babel. The people of Babel, under Nimrod's leadership, chose to build the tower of bricks. This choice of material demonstrates an important spiritual truth because bricks symbolize human effort without God in contrast to stones created by

God. The bricks would not hold together and so the people used mortar made out of tar as a binding (*see* Genesis 11:3). This is the way man, by his human effort, builds his system. God's Kingdom, in contrast, is bound together by a willing submitting to God's authority and results in peace and love. The human system represented by Babel is an idolatrous system, both religious and political. It is a mirror image of God's Truth and therefore backwards, and it is ultimately without spiritual validity. Such a system produces conditions similar to what B. F. Skinner describes as an establishment with an elite ruling clique, whose members virtually deify themselves and *enslave* the rest of mankind. Under this kind of world system, Satan binds people and takes away their uniqueness, dignity, and freedom of choice.

A monument to mankind. God observed the collective efforts of humans to build their own system apart from Him. To deal with the situation, God brought division through the introduction of different languages. This made it impossible for the people in Nimrod's empire to complete the tower, leaving it incomplete as an appropriate monument to mankind apart from God.

Man's system apart from God may look exciting because it appeals to the senses. It may also seem secure but as surely as in Babel, God will either bring division to it or it will destroy itself, whereas God's Incredible Plan will never be stopped.

We are all aware today of the brilliant achievements of modern-day man—inventions such as the laser beam, which is being used medically and in industry, and is accomplishing great good. But its destructive capabilities are also being developed in modern weaponry. Laser beams can be used to blind or annihilate the enemy in a war.

Which will the laser be used for—to alleviate illness or destroy mankind? Man apart from God has no absolute value system of right or wrong and there will always be the selfish opportunist, like Nimrod, who will force *his* life-style, *his* kingdom plan, on all the rest of his fellow men. The result is predictable since history is replete with the Genghis Khans and Adolf Hitlers and their resultant destruction.

Abraham: Man of Faith

The journey through the Bible takes us now to the time of God's ancient leaders called the patriarchs. The first patriarch lived in Ur of the Chaldees (area of Babel) when God called him out of it to start a race of God's people who would claim His land. This man was called Abram. He was to become the "father of those who believe" (Romans 4:11 LB).

Abram With the Willing Heart.   God broke into the world system and called one man out of it, promising to make him the father of a great nation and through him to bless the nations of the world. Abram came from an idolatrous city where his family worshiped other gods (*see* Joshua 24:2). In Abram's call, we see how the all-knowing God finds what kind of person He wants as a leader in His Kingdom. In Abram, God found a *willing heart* and brought Abram gradually, step by step, into a personal relationship with Himself.

Abram took his family and all his belongings to Haran, but his response was partial in that he remained in Haran for at least five years. After five years he left Haran, at the age of seventy-five, and moved into Canaan the Promised Land, the real estate God had claimed (*see* Genesis 12:4). There Abram offered his first sacrifice to God at Shechem (*see* Genesis 12:6, 7).

God had promised *to show* Abram the Promised Land. After Abram responded to God's call by faith, God then promised *to give* the land to his seed. When he pitched his tent at Bethel, a name meaning "house of God," Abram was told to walk around the land and claim it for his descendents who would be as numerous as the stars in the sky (*see* Genesis 13:14–17; 15:5). Abram believed God and God considered him righteous because of his *faith*. The descendents of Abram became a new race of people who were at first called Israelites and later Jews. They were called to be God's Chosen People.

God's Chosen People.   God's strategy involves a literal piece of real estate inhabited by His Chosen People. This is not to say that all in God's Land were His followers, nor does it mean that every person outside of His Land was opposed to God. God deals with all people on the basis of how they respond to Him personally. He deals with His Chosen People individually and on the basis of how they respond to His plan for them as a nation. He deals with the nations of the world on the basis of how they relate to His Chosen People.

The reasons God selected a special race to be His Chosen People are of great significance to all the world:

1. To record and preserve God's written Word through time (*see* Romans 3:2).
2. That through the Chosen Race, the Messiah would come, the One who would defeat Satan and reconcile man to God in His Redemptive Plan (*see* Galatians 3:14–16).
3. They were charged to be a light among the nations. Many people feel that God was playing favorites by choosing a people when, in fact, their choice involves special service to all peoples.

The significance of this strategy is amply demonstrated by Satan's continuing effort to destroy the Jewish race in every age. God's Sovereign Power is historically proved by the very fact of their continued existence as a racial entity, even while dispersed over the entire world.

Another important statement which was made by God at the time He called Abram has remained true throughout history: He would bless those who bless His people and curse those who curse His people (*see* Genesis 12:3).

Abraham and Sarah. Abraham and Sarah, as God now called Abram and his wife, were childless even though they had been promised many descendents. Instead of waiting for God's timing, however, Sarah took things into her own hands when she gave Hagar, her maid, to Abraham so that he might have a son. Sarah's happy home was upset by the very means she used to fulfill God's promise. Our human nature does not like to wait for God's timing. Instead, we take things into our own hands, helping God along.

The result was envy, strife, and finally, an act of cruelty on Sarah's part. Sarah was harsh with Hagar and poor Hagar fled to the wilderness where the angel of the Lord said, "Return to

Sarah. You are going to bear a son and you shall call his name Ishmael" (*see* Genesis 16:11). Ishmael was to have many important descendents himself, which today are known as the Arab nations.

God reminded Abraham that His promise of a son had always been through Sarah, his wife, and that they should wait for that event according to God's timing. When God calls Himself "the God of Abraham," it is not because Abraham was always consistent in his walk of faith but rather because Abraham allowed God to work in his life. This fact can be of great comfort to us when we have failed in our walk with God. He does not discard us or put us on probation, but continues working with us until we can see that His plan for our life is the best one.

Isaac

Sarah finally conceived a child, Isaac—a miracle at her age—and became a mother, thus fulfilling God's promise. Because of strife in the household, Sarah insisted that Hagar and Ishmael be sent away. Abraham gave them provisions and sadly sent them off, after God had said He would care for them and make a nation of Ishmael's descendents.

God's Substitute. When Isaac was about fourteen years old, God asked of Abraham the ultimate response of faith. He asked Abraham to sacrifice his miraculous son as a burnt offering. Trusting God, Abraham obeyed and started the three-day journey to Mount Moriah with Isaac, his son, through whom God had promised blessing to the whole world. This promise would have been humanly impossible had Isaac been sacrificed, but Abraham believed God even to the extent of believing that God would raise Isaac from the dead (*see* Hebrews 11:19). This amazing faith qualified Abraham to be the "father of those who believe" (Romans 4:11 LB). Here, also, God rejected the use of human sacrifice as other nations practiced. God revealed several more truths about forgiveness:

1. The burnt offering pictures the sentence of death, which has been pronounced on all men, since God cannot tolerate sin in His presence.

2. What God demands, God provides. Therefore, *He* provides a Substitute Sacrifice, One who will die in our place (*see* Figure 4).
3. The Substitute is His only begotten Son Jesus the Messiah, whom Isaac prepictured perfectly.
4. Mount Moriah is in Jerusalem where the Messiah, the Perfect Substitute, sacrificed Himself for all mankind.

Apparently Abraham understood these spiritual truths as he offered up the substitute ram which God provided. Jesus said as much, more than two thousand years later. Abraham loved God more than his own life and was willing to place Isaac in His hands rather than cling to Isaac and bargain with God.

Jacob

The next man who was willing to follow God was Jacob, one of Isaac's sons. Between the twins, Jacob and Esau, Jacob was not the one whom man would normally choose for God's purposes. His very name means "supplanter and deceiver" (*see* Genesis 25:26).

Twin Brothers. Jacob and Esau were twins but were very different from each other. Esau, because he was the older twin, possessed the birthright. Esau was world-system oriented and one day he became so hungry after a hunting trip that he sold his birthright for a bowl of stew. His birthright was a God-given privilege to become the head of the race but he thought so little of it that he was willing to trade it for some stew.

Later, Jacob and his mother tricked Esau out of his father's blessing. Fearing his brother's anger, Jacob fled to Haran where he worked for his Uncle Laban. Throughout these years, God pursued Jacob, seeing in him a *willing heart*.

The Wrestling Match. On his way back to Canaan many years later, Jacob wrestled all night with God in the form of a man at a place called Peniel, located close to the Sea of Galilee. The reason he wrestled all night is expressed by his saying, "I will not let you go until you bless me" (Genesis 32:26 LB). That is what God wanted—Jacob's complete surrender to His will. At that point,

God changed Jacob's name to Israel, which means "prince of God." He was to become the father of the twelve tribes of Israel. In the morning, Jacob emerged renamed and blessed. He was a truly changed man after his encounter at Peniel, the place which means the "face of God."

Israel's Sons.   Joseph was one of Israel's twelve sons. Because he was Israel's favorite, his brothers became jealous of him. Also, Joseph's dreams, which he told to his brothers, always pictured the brothers bowing in obeisance to him. The very thought of this infuriated his brothers, so they conspired together and sold Joseph into slavery to the Midianites for twenty pieces of silver. They dipped his multicolored coat into blood and showed it to Israel, convincing him of Joseph's death. The brothers' cruel deception convinced their brokenhearted father that Joseph was killed, but God was with him to protect him (*see* Genesis 37).

We will see how Joseph became an important link in God's plan for His Chosen Nation.

5

Toward the Promised Land

The journey of the Israelites to the Promised Land was probably the greatest journey ever taken. Every journey must have a beginning, of course, and this journey began in Egypt, with God's Chosen People enslaved in the service of the Pharaohs.

Bondage in the World System

God's care of Joseph was so thorough that he experienced a miraculous rise from prison to palace, where he became second in importance to the Pharaoh. This rise to power and prominence in Egypt was an important part of God's Incredible Plan because it resulted in Joseph bringing his entire family—seventy people—to Egypt. The reason for the move was to preserve them from famine and to unite them once more, but the result was also to take them out of God's Land and into the world system. Joseph, in observing the whole process, commented later to his brothers, "As far as I am concerned, God turned into good what you meant for evil, for he brought me to this high position I have today so that I could save the lives of many people" (Genesis 50:20 LB). God caused the famine to keep His Chosen People from intermarrying with the Canaanites who were so depraved. In Egypt the Hebrews lived separately and became a race.

As the Hebrew people multiplied from that original seventy and prospered in Egypt, the succeeding Pharaohs became afraid of them and enslaved them. Finally, the ruling Pharaoh introduced measures to stop their growth by killing all the boy babies. When the bondage of the Hebrew people became intolerable, they remembered God and cried out to Him and, true to His promise, God broke into history to protect and preserve His Kingdom. We are no different today. How often we wait to call on God until all our plans have failed and we are in desperate straits. God has not changed, either. He just as graciously answers our cry and as faithfully delivers us.

Moses.   During this dark time of bondage, God prepared a Hebrew baby named Moses who would deliver the nation of Israel. To protect him from the Pharaoh's edict to kill all male babies, his mother hid Moses in a basket on the river where the Pharaoh's daughter found him. With his sister Miriam secretly watching, Pharaoh's daughter pulled the basket containing Moses out of the water and took the baby home to raise him as her own son. So it came about that God's man was raised in Pharaoh's court with all the advantages of the finest education and culture available in the world system.

Moses, by faith, chose to identify with his own people and in doing so, he was willing to choose what God had planned for him, rather than to own all the rich treasures of Egypt (*see* Hebrews 11:24–26). By an act of his own will, Moses chose to be part of the People of God rather than the world system.

Preparation to Be God's Leader.   Because of his identification with the Hebrew people, and by his killing an Egyptian, Moses was forced to flee Egypt. He went to the far side of the desert at Midian, where he shepherded flocks and married Zipporah. It was there that God, through the burning bush, called Moses to lead God's People.

Moses was a hesitant recruit when God commissioned him to lead the people of Israel out of Egypt. Moses claimed he was a nobody and that he had no message, no authority, and no eloquence. Moses finally said, "Not me, Lord, send someone else" (*see* Exodus 4:13); he was understandably afraid. God answered by promising His Power and Provision. In addition, God told Moses that his message was to be, "I AM has sent me!" (*see* Exodus 3:14). I AM was used to mean the name of Jehovah God, or Yahweh.

The kind of people God chooses are those whose hearts are willing. Isn't it encouraging to us when we realize that God doesn't demand the greatest mind or top-notch ability in His leaders! *He* has the Power and gives direction and all we need to do is believe and submit to His leadership.

The Plagues and the Passover.   When Pharaoh was unwilling to release the Hebrew people from their bondage, God used plagues as a means of persuading him to send the children of Israel out of Egypt. This miracle of plagues was necessary both to make the Jews willing to leave and to force Pharaoh to send them.

After a series of plagues in which Pharaoh refused to repent, the last and worst plague was decreed in which the firstborn son of each family in Egypt was to die. This plague not only displayed God's judgment of Pharaoh but was also an explicit picture of God's Redemptive Plan. Each believing Hebrew family killed an unblemished lamb and sprinkled its blood on the top and sides of the door frame. The blood was to protect that home from the death of the firstborn son. The lamb was to be eaten as the people were standing and ready to leave. The ceremony of the Passover is celebrated by Jewish families even today.

The Passover, in each detail, adds to our understanding of God's River of Truth (*see* Figure 4). The personal application of the blood to the doorposts, *by faith*, made that home a refuge from the judgment of death. God, seeing the blood, passed over that home. The blood is significant as a symbol in that it is the necessary element of life in all flesh. In His Redemptive Plan, God uses *blood* as an atonement for our souls and forgiveness of sin (*see* Leviticus 17:11, Hebrews 9:22).

The Great Escape

Pharaoh, because of the last plague, finally ordered Moses to take the children of Israel and leave Egypt. When Pharaoh later changed his mind, God held him to his decision, in order to free the Hebrew people from slavery and demonstrate His Power through a miracle of escape.

Pharaoh pursued the Israelites with his chariots and found them trapped, with their backs to the Red Sea. There was no human way to escape. It was useless to run before the chariots of Egypt. It was also useless to fight because they were an unarmed slave force of men, women, and children. Miraculously, God opened up a pathway through the midst of the Red Sea and commanded His People to march forward on dry ground to the other side. When the Hebrew people were safely across, the returning waters destroyed Pharaoh and his army.

This miracle of escape is used to demonstrate God's Power and concern for His People but it also discloses how people either rely on, or fail to rely on, God's Power. Moses knew God personally and believed in His Power. The people, however, failed to trust God. They looked at the enemy and their circumstances and, not trusting God, blamed Moses for their predicament. Moses, on the other hand, trusted God and knew that He would keep His promise to bring them out of Egypt. How often we react to our circumstances as though they were in control rather than Almighty God. Moses told the people to stand and watch how wonderfully the Lord would rescue them. God did just that.

The Wilderness Trip

God led His People out of the most powerful kingdom on earth and into the wilderness on one of the longest and most unusual trips ever to occur. This trip resulted in God revealing to His People many truths about Himself and about His ways for their lives.

God's Provisions.   God provided for His People in many special ways that show His recognition of both spiritual and physical needs. In one of these, God led the people through the wilderness with a pillar of cloud by day and a pillar of fire by night. The pillar was a cover to keep them cool by day and to give warmth and light during the cold desert nights (*see* Psalms 105:39). Even more important, this cloud, which was called the Shekinah glory, was visible evidence of God's Presence with them. The Shekinah glory was with the people, guiding them, protecting them, and progressively teaching them about God and His **Holiness,** as we will see (*see* Figure 3).

God provided for every physical need of His People as well as their spiritual needs. He sent them bread from heaven in a daily supply called manna. The Lord reminded them that just as He supplied their physical need for bread, so He supplies the Bread of Life by giving us His Word, which we need to read and obey (*see* Deuteronomy 8:3; Matthew 4:4; John 6).

The wilderness wanderings picture in many ways our spiritual pilgrimage, from the world system and its enslavement, into God's Kingdom. We are brought out of our enslavement to sin by the *Power* of God. The pilgrimage to God's Rest (the Promised Land) may be long or short, depending on whether or not we follow the "cloud" of God's leading.

The Israelites were finally led to Mount Sinai according to instructions God had given to Moses when He first called him in the burning bush (*see* Exodus 3:12).

God's Value System.   At Mount Sinai, God gave them His Law which included the Ten Commandments, and in so doing revealed His Value System. These are the reasons God gave the Law to His People:

1. To give the Israelites a separate national identity and to provide a workable civil government. This is why there are multitudes of seemingly unimportant rules.

2. The Law reveals a perfect ethics system and is therefore a picture of God's character. The intent of this Law is most clearly described in the Sermon on the Mount (*see* Matthew 5–7), in which Jesus took the Old Testament Law and interpreted it from God's point of view. There, Jesus said, "You have heard . . . you shall not commit murder . . . but I say to you that everyone who is angry with his brother shall be in danger of hell's fire" (*see* Matthew 5:21, 22). "You have heard . . . you shall not commit adultery . . . but I say that everyone who looks on a woman to lust for her has committed adultery with her already in his heart" (*see* Matthew 5:27, 28). In summary, Jesus goes on to say, "You are to be perfect as your heavenly Father is perfect" (*see* Matthew 5:48). If you and I really read the Sermon on the Mount honestly, there is no one of us who can believe he has kept the law or will ever be able to keep it.

What Jesus did was explain God's perfect Law and in doing so, revealed God's Value System. Jesus showed us in the Sermon on the Mount that God really does not judge so much the external performance of the Law as He does the condition of a person's heart. Realistically we would have to agree. The condition of our hearts is deceitful, as Jeremiah the prophet verifies when he states, "The heart is the most deceitful thing there is, and desperately wicked . . ." (Jeremiah 17:9 LB).

The significance of this second reason for the Law is there is absolutely no way to measure up to God's Value System. God's Value System is perfection, either 100 percent perfection or 100 percent failure (*see* James 2:10). God does not grade on the curve! There is no sin so little that God will overlook it, and no sin so great that God has not made provision for it.

God's Value System is in sharp contrast with the values of the world system, which does grade on a curve. The world system adheres to the values of "doing the best you can with what you have" or religiously, "God helps those who help themselves," and "After all, nobody can be perfect!" Such a value system deifies man and belittles God, bringing Him down to little more than an "escape" for a tight spot if all else fails. The great deceiver, Satan, promotes this belief so that man will rationalize the guilt he feels and will not recognize his need for forgiveness. Not recognizing the Holiness of God, man need not face up to his own hopeless condition.

The second reason for the Law, then, is to help us understand our own need. This is described in Romans 3:20, where Paul states, "His laws serve only to make us see that we are sinners" (LB).

3. The third reason the Law was given was to condemn sin. God makes it very clear that sin has caused the separation between Himself and man and must therefore be judged (*see* Isaiah 59:2). Even our most righteous deeds are but filthy rags in God's sight (*see* Isaiah 64:6). Keeping the Law, it should be remembered, is like forging a chain. It is only as strong as its weakest link and breaking the Law in one point, even one evil thought, is in God's Value System equivalent to breaking all of it (*see* James 2:10). The condemnation or judgment for breaking the Law is clear: God's only wage for sin is eternal death (*see* Romans 6:23).

4. The fourth reason for the Law is that it diagnoses man's problem which is *rebellion*. The Law does not change human nature or provide a solution to man's problem; rather, it serves as an X ray of the problem. It reveals the problem but does not solve it. In fact, it produces rebellion within people (*see* Romans 5:20; 7:7, 8).

5. A fifth reason for the Law is that it shows man the necessity of depending on God's Provision for his sinful condition. When

people understand the full meaning of the Law, they stop trying to be self-righteous by their own human effort and cry out to God for help. Sin was forgiven in the Old Testament only by trusting in God and using His Provision in the temporary sacrificial system (*see* Hebrews 10:4). *Why would God give His People the sacrificial system if He expected them to keep the Law?* The Law points them to God but access to God has always been on the basis of *faith.* If we allow God's Law to do its job in our hearts, it will drive us to the Messiah, who is God's Provision, the One Perfect Sacrifice (*see* Hebrews 10:12).

The Tabernacle: God's First House

God established the sacrificial system to enable people to understand how He, the Creator God, had to do all that was necessary for people to be reconciled or brought back to God. This provision for reconciliation centered in the Tabernacle, the place where God and His People met. By symbolically dwelling in this building, God demonstrated His original purpose for man in Eden, which was to live in them and to walk among them (*see* 2 Corinthians 6:16).

The Tabernacle, called the Tent of the Testimony, was a clear picture of God's Redemptive Plan in its structure, furnishings, and the role of the priesthood as well as the offerings and sacrifices. A detailed explanation of the symbolism of the Tabernacle is presented in Appendix B.

The Day of Atonement. The main sacrifice for sin was made on the Day of Atonement and pictured the way a person was to approach God. The priest, who at this time mediated between man and God, symbolically placed all the sins of the Israelites on an animal's head. Then after the animal was killed as a substitute for the people, the priest took blood from it and went through the Holy Place into a cubicle called the Holy of Holies (*see* Figure 5). There he sprinkled the blood on the "mercy seat" of the ark of the covenant (*see* Leviticus 16:15). The "ark" was a small, wooden box, overlaid with gold, and had a lid (mercy seat) of pure gold. On the lid were two cherubim (angelic beings) with wings touching, looking down on the ark (*see* Figure 5). Between

the cherubim hovered the Shekinah glory, the Holy Presence of God.

The ark contained three things:

1. A jar of manna—to show God's Provision for sustaining life, which the people rejected (*see* Numbers 21).
2. Aaron's rod of leadership—to demonstrate God's appointed authority which the people rebelled against (*see* Numbers 16).
3. The Ten Commandments—to reveal God's Law, which the people broke (*see* Exodus 20).

Therefore these articles symbolized both God's Love and care, and man's sin and self-centeredness. When the priest sprinkled the blood of the animal on the mercy seat, it symbolically "covered" the three articles within the ark (*see* Leviticus 16:13).

The wonderful truth taught in the sacrificial system was that the sinner need not die. Instead, the substitute unblemished animal died. The blood was the symbol of that death. The sinner deserved the death but it was the innocent animal that died in the place of the sinner. It may be remembered that God had told Adam and Eve that if they chose to separate from Him, they would inevitably die because God Himself is the only source of Eternal Life. Without Eternal Life from God, eternal death must follow. This sentence applied to all their descendents and therefore to all of mankind.

In the sacrificial system, God demonstrated that He recognized the guilt of the sinner and although He did not ignore or overlook it, He was willing to bear it Himself. In so doing, He committed Himself to be the unblemished Lamb of God (*see* John 1:29), to bear Himself the death penalty which He had decreed for all mankind. In this way, God portrayed His reconciling **LOVE** to the Israelites and revealed His Redemptive Plan to bring an end to the separation which sin had caused. Separation from God cannot be restored by human righteousness or self-effort on man's part. All God asks from man is **Faith**—believing in Him, responding to His Love, and accepting His Eternal Life. That is His will. That is His plan.

The Mosaic Covenant

Here at Mount Sinai, God made His covenant with His People, an agreement that is often called the Mosaic Covenant. In this covenant, God told the Hebrew people that He would bless them as His Chosen People if they functioned in accordance with His moral, civil, and ceremonial laws. These laws were designed to hedge them in from the immoral, idolatrous, pagan cultures of the world system and to reveal to them God's viewpoint.

Moses the Mediator

The Israelites agreed to keep the Mosaic Covenant but while Moses was still on Mount Sinai, they disowned their God and broke their agreement with Him. Aaron, at the people's request, made a golden calf which the people worshiped, thus reverting back to the same idolatry the Egyptians practiced. Their gross idolatry was soon followed by all kinds of sexual immorality. While Moses was still on Mount Sinai, God told him, *"Your*

people have defiled themselves . . . I see they are stubborn and
rebellious and deserve My judgment" (*see* Exodus 32:9, 10 LB).

Moses, in his God-appointed role as mediator, pleaded for the
people. In this dialogue, Moses stressed three truths:

1. God had delivered the people from slavery because of His
   Love and not because the people deserved it.
2. God's character was at stake before the watching world.
3. God had delivered the Hebrew people because of His promises to Abraham, and since He is faithful He cannot deny
   Himself and His Word.

God listened to the pleading of Moses and in so doing, an
important truth became apparent. Moses fulfilled his role as
God's appointed mediator, a role which pictures the forthcoming
Glorified Mediator, Jesus Christ, who would reconcile sinful man
to a just God. Through the intercession of Moses, Israel repented,
and again became *God's* People through whom God was to reveal
Himself to Planet Earth.

We today, looking back, may wonder why God so patiently
continued to use Israel as His Chosen People, the ones through
whom His Incredible Plan was unfolding. The reason becomes
clear as we honestly examine our own rebellious hearts. Do we
deserve God's Love? Have we ever selfishly put our goals
("idols") of materialism, position, and power above God? Do we
really love and worship God with *all* our heart, and with *all* our
soul, and *all* our might? (*see* Deuteronomy 6:5).

The Faithful Two and the Fearful Ten

After Mount Sinai, the Shekinah glory (God's Presence) led the
Israelites to Kadesh-barnea, where Moses sent twelve spies into
the Promised Land. The spies went as far as Hebron, returning
with a huge bunch of grapes and fruit and telling about the land
flowing with milk and honey. They also told of the walled cities
and giants in the land. Ten of the twelve spies were fearful and
convinced the people not to trust God even though God had miraculously brought them up out of Egypt for this very moment: to
enter into Canaan, the Land He had promised to Abraham for his
descendents.

Joshua and Caleb, the remaining two spies, trusted God and wanted to go into the Land. Fear overcame faith, however, and the Israelites refused to enter the Promised Land. Instead, they reverted to grumbling, blaming Moses and God for their condition. This presents a true picture of the steps of unbelief in man. Not claiming and enjoying what God has promised to give always results in blaming Him for circumstances and problems.

The Result of Not Trusting God

The lack of trust in God resulted in forty years of wandering in the desert. The generation that did not believe God was not allowed to enter the Promised Land, with the exception of Joshua and Caleb.

Before Moses died, he appointed Joshua as his successor according to God's instructions. Moses also gave the Israelites some wonderful advice by setting before them Eternal Life or eternal death. He told them to "choose to love the Lord your God and obey Him and cling to Him, for He is your Eternal **Life**" (*see* Deuteronomy 30:20).

Moses then climbed Mount Nebo where God showed him the Promised Land spread out before him. This was the Land God had promised to give to Abraham's descendents, God's Land on Planet Earth. Moses died and God Himself buried him. There has never been another prophet like Moses, for the Lord talked to him mouth to mouth (*see* Numbers 12:8) and, at God's command, he performed amazing miracles which were never equalled until the coming of Jesus Christ (*see* Deuteronomy 34:12 LB). The children of Israel observed God's acts but Moses *knew* God's ways (*see* Psalms 103:7).

The Promised Land

Joshua assumed leadership after the death of Moses and first determined that information would be needed about the Promised Land before occupying the territory. He decided to send two spies into Jericho, a key city in the land of Canaan just across the river Jordan. The spies not only obtained the needed information but in the process were saved from death by a remarkable woman.

Rahab's Saving Faith.   Rahab was the proprietress of an inn where the spies stayed. Although a prostitute, she had come to realize that the Creator God of the heavens and the earth was the God of Israel. The thing that convinced her was the miraculous way He had rolled back the Red Sea to make a path for the Israelites to walk through on dry land, and then destroyed their enemies behind them with the returning of the waters. She believed in God, knowing only of His Power and leadership of Israel.

Rahab protected the spies by hiding them from her townsfolk, and at night she let them out of her window and down to safety by a scarlet rope. Rahab believed that the city would fall to Israel and she asked the spies to save her family and herself. The spies agreed, and told her to place the scarlet rope in her window as an identifying mark which would be used to protect her and her household from death. This scarlet rope and the safety of Rahab's household was another picture of the Passover, in that God protected those who placed faith in Him.

Rahab not only became a believer but also became an ancestress of the kingly line of Judah. This was the line of ancestry of King David, from which the King of Kings was to come. More important, her *faith* was from her heart which, regardless of background, is always counted by God as righteousness (*see* Genesis 15:6).

Crossing the River Jordan.   At last the Israelites crossed the Jordan River into the Promised Land and God allowed them to do it in the same miraculous way they had crossed the Red Sea in the beginning of their journey. The crossing occurred during the early-spring flooding but God rolled back the river to provide a dry path and Joshua led the people safely across to the west bank.

Joshua needed a strategy to take the Promised Land, so as soon as he crossed the Jordan River, he looked over the city of Jericho. While walking alone mapping out his strategy, a Man with a drawn sword appeared before him and said, "I am the Commander-in-Chief of the Lord's army. . . . Take off your shoes, for this is holy ground" (Joshua 5:14, 15 LB; *see also*

Exodus 3:5 LB). The miraculous Man was the Lord and He mapped out a strategy for Joshua which was to be the Battle of Jericho.

The Battle of Jericho. Jericho was a walled city with tightly shut defenses. Rather than storm the impregnable walls, however, Joshua followed God's instructions and marched around the city, blowing trumpets and shouting. At God's command, the walls of Jericho crumbled to the ground and the people of Israel poured into the city from every direction, completely destroying it.

The destruction of Jericho and the subsequent campaign throughout Canaan was the fulfillment of God's judgment on the wickedness and corruption of the nations living in Canaan. Hundreds of years before, God had told Abraham that the wickedness of Canaan was not yet ready for His judgment (*see* Genesis 15:16). This statement shows that God is always patient and waiting, much longer than seems necessary, for man to repent and turn to Him (*see* 2 Peter 3:9). Some never do. The Canaanites, like the people of Noah's time, had become so corrupt that God could no longer withhold His just judgment. In this case, God used the Israelites as His means of judgment on the Canaanites, just as the heavenly Man with the drawn sword indicated would happen. God was the leader of the Israelites in defeating the highly fortified city of Jericho.

Lessons From History

The history of the nation of Israel demonstrates pictures of us as individuals in our walk with God. We are often willing to seek God's help in an impossible situation (such as Jericho) but depend on self-sufficiency with small problems. God, however, desires to be the Commander-in-Chief of every area of our lives. He will then be responsible for the direction of our lives, and the result will be fulfillment as well as peace in our innermost beings.

The conquest of Canaan took between five and seven years. During that time, each tribe was given the responsibility of cleaning up its own area, a task which they never completely accomplished. The tribes disobeyed God by failing to remove the Canaanite sins and idolatries from the land and these unresolved

Canaanite sins infected the nation of Israel for generations to follow.

There is much for us to learn by observing Joshua's life which was a steady walk with God, first as a humble member of, and then as the leader of, the Israelites. In his farewell address to Israel, Joshua summed up the choice which is open to people of every age. He told them their choice was whether they would worship God and God alone or worship the false gods of the Canaanites. If they chose Jehovah God who had brought them out of Egypt and into the Promised Land, He would bless them and make them prosper. But if the people chose against Him and pursued their own idolatries, God's protection would cease. Joshua closed his farewell address by declaring, "As for me and my family, we will serve the Lord" (Joshua 24:15 LB).

The people of Israel agreed to worship the Lord only and Joshua made them witnesses to their own choice. This agreement or covenant occurred at a place called Shechem which was Abraham's first place of sacrifice. At the age of 110 years, Joshua died. Throughout his life, Israel had walked faithfully with God, but after his death a gradual turning away from God began which was to result in chaos.

6

The Rise and Fall
of the Jewish Empire

These are the years, which bring to a high point the Jewish Empire in the Promised Land. During the next several hundred years, we shall see God form a nation from a group of wandering Hebrew tribes. We shall see that nation in the Golden Age of David and Solomon become a mighty kingdom, only to observe that kingdom divide and be carried into the captivity of a neighboring power.

The Era of the Judges

After conquering the Promised Land, the people of Israel began to intermarry with the remaining Canaanites. This resulted in worshiping false gods and the practice of various forms of sexual perversion. The Bible summarizes the prevailing attitude of this period of decay and disobedience by stating, ". . . everyone did what was right in his own eyes" (Judges 21:25).

The effect of ignoring God's ways for man was clearly demonstrated during this era. When man does what is right in his eyes, without reference to God's Absolutes, decay and confusion always results. This is consistent with our understanding that Satan, ruler of the world system and God's archenemy, desires chaos and anarchy in order to undermine God's law and order. Because Satan is the great deceiver, he has no problem convincing *autonomous* man, apart from God, to "go down the pleasant road which he thinks is right but which ends in death" (*see* Proverbs 16:25). This is the kind of "everyday existentialism" epitomized today by "doing your own thing." The result, for both individuals and the society, is decay and disintegration.

During this period of chaos and confusion, God raised up Judges through whom He spoke. Because of the decay within, Israel also fell easy prey to enemies outside the nation. First one

nation and then another invaded and made portions of Israel their
vassal state, then God would use some of the Judges to lead the
people in defense of Israel against the invading nations.

Sometimes when the people were in great difficulty, they would
turn to God and He would raise up a Judge, such as Gideon, to
speak to the people and lead them. After the immediate peril was
past, however, the people soon forgot and turned away from God.
This attitude is not unlike the "foxhole religion" of contemporary
times. We can so easily cry out to God for help when we are
desperate, and then so quickly forget Him when the immediate
terror is past.

Samuel: The Last Judge.   The last Judge of Israel lived in an era
of unusual political activity. The people of Israel, after several
hundred years and against the will of God, were demanding a king
like all of the other nations. In reality, they were asking for a
political institutional system which would allow them to function
without relying on God. They reasoned that a king would be
placed in godlike authority where he could be seen by the people
and would also offer greater protection and be more easily followed. A succession of kings could also be established so there
would be no need to trust God to raise up a judge. This tendency
for people to choose a well-organized system in preference to
reliance on God can be observed throughout history and continues today.

Samuel, the last and the greatest of the Judges, was distressed
by the people's request for a king and went to the Lord for advice.
God assured him that the people were not rejecting Samuel but
that Israel was rejecting *God* as their Supreme Ruler. They had
continually followed after other gods and now they wanted to be
even more like the world around them by having a king.

God granted the desire of the people to have a king, knowing
they would learn through their own willfulness. He told Samuel,
however, to warn the people about what it would be like to have a
king. Samuel warned them of taxation and of conscription of men
and women, saying it would be like slavery all over again. The
people insisted on having a king, however, saying he could gov-
ern them and lead them into battle (*see* 1 Samuel 8:20).

God was to use even the monarchy for His purpose and His plan. It was through this line of ancestry, through the tribe of Judah, that the King of Kings was to come, demonstrating God's ultimate Sovereignty. God, being Sovereign and also gracious, uses even our mistakes and wrong choices to work together for our good and His glory (*see* Romans 8:28).

Three Kings

The nation of Israel received its kings. Three of these kings are of unusual interest in understanding the development of Israel as a nation and God's will for His People. These kings are Saul, David, and Solomon.

King Saul. Saul, the first of three kings of the monarchy, was anointed by Samuel himself. Saul began his rule with a humble attitude but soon his victories made him proud and he became disobedient to God. Little by little, one step at a time, Saul became more self-willed until finally God set him aside as ruler.

Saul's crucial act of self-will involved his intentions, or his heart attitude, about the right of God to rule in his life. Because of his success and power, Saul set himself above God. After turning away from following God, Saul then offered a sacrifice instead of waiting for Samuel. The act of Saul in offering a religious sacrifice, which under other circumstances would have been acceptable if Saul's attitude had been one of willingness to follow God, was particularly offensive to God. When Samuel arrived, he rebuked Saul's self-will and pointed out that obedience is far better than a religous practice. He observed that God sees the heart and that outward religious performance without inward faith is the greatest offense to God. Saul was unwilling to accept God's will for his life, and finally he resorted to visiting a witch for supernatural help, an act clearly forbidden by God.

King David. When Saul turned his back on God, God directed Samuel to anoint David as the second king of Israel. When David was anointed, he was still a shepherd boy, but he was destined to become Israel's greatest king. God explained that He had selected David because of the integrity of his heart. God brought

David out of tending sheep to "feed His people" and gave him
Israel as his inheritance, because of the willingness of David's
heart (*see* Psalms 78:70, 71).

David was described as "a man after God's own heart" (*see* 1
Samuel 13:14; Acts 13:22). The secret to understanding the nature
of David's heart is in his love for the Word of God and his living
dependence on God's promises. David was both a mighty warrior
and a gifted musician-poet and he wrote and sang many beautiful
psalms, expressing his worship and praise to God.

David exalted God above all, recognizing His holy character
and Power. Like Moses, David believed God and was able to see
every obstacle from God's viewpoint. An early example of his
attitude was revealed when David was a teenager and faced the
giant, Goliath. David shouted the challenge, saying that the Lord
does not depend on man's weapons or means to fulfill His plan
and that God's plan was for Israel and the whole world to know
that *He is God* (*see* 1 Samuel 17:45–47). David killed Goliath with
a sling and smooth stone, then the Israelites routed the Philistine
army. In the process, God's name and His holy Power were vindicated.

During his reign as king, David wanted to build a permanent
house for God. The site he chose was on Mount Moriah, the same
spot where Abraham journeyed to offer up Isaac (which was described in chapter 4). Instead, God gave the task of building the
Temple to David's son, Solomon, but He made an unconditional
covenant with David. God promised David (1) an eternal kingdom, (2) an eternal throne, and (3) an eternal Descendent. What
God was promising was *His* answer to David's request. David
wanted to build God an earthly house but God replied that He
was going to build David's "house" into an eternal one, with his
Greater Son Jesus ruling forever (*see* 1 Chronicles 17:11–14).
When Jesus, the King of Kings, came, He acknowledged that He
was "the root and the offspring of David . . . ." (Revelation
22:16).

Later in life David sinned grievously and Nathan the prophet
was sent by God to face David with his sin. David agreed with
God, admitting his sin and accepting the discipline of his loving
heavenly Father. Because David had a personal love relationship

with God he knew he was forgiven, so he was able to walk on with God in close fellowship. In Psalm 51 David reveals his clear understanding of God's Redemptive Plan when he asks to be cleansed "whiter than snow" as God blots out all his sins and creates a clean heart within.

King Solomon.   Solomon reached many worldly goals as king of Israel, but his most significant achievement was the building of the first Temple. Following instructions given by his father, David, Solomon patterned the Temple after the Tabernacle (which is described in Appendix B) and built it on Mount Moriah. The Temple was constructed of hewn stone, fitted together at the Temple site, without the sound of a hammer. Eighty thousand men cut stone in Solomon's quarries, thirty thousand men cut the cedar, and there were seventy thousand additional craftsmen. The Temple was magnificent in every detail and the ark of the covenant was placed in the Holy of Holies (the innermost part of the Temple) with great rejoicing on the day of dedication. God's Shekinah glory hovered over the ark as a sign of His Presence in their midst.

When Solomon became king, he asked for and received from God the gift of a wise and discerning heart. During his forty-year reign, there was peace and prosperity. He also wrote the Book of Proverbs, which sets forth spiritual wisdom and truth in practical and applicable sayings for family life and business.

Tragically, Solomon in later years did not practice the wisdom he had been given. He married many wives and became enslaved to luxury and wealth. He overtaxed the people and his opulence produced decadence in the kingdom, weakening it. Even more serious was his sin of allowing his wives to turn his heart away from Jehovah God to their false idols. The nation as a whole followed Solomon's example, even with the glorious new Temple in their midst.

Israel's worship of God became more formal and ritualistic through the years instead of increasing in fervor and desire to follow God. The Temple and *its* glory became their god rather than Almighty God, whose Presence hovered over the Temple. We always seem to worship the seen rather than the Unseen. We are often subtly caught up in "things" which are the evidence of our own achievement rather than worshiping the One who gives us our ability and sustains our very life.

Apparently, at the end of Solomon's life he wrote the Book of Ecclesiastes. In it, he described how things appear "under the sun" or without God's viewpoint (Ecclesiastes 4:1). Solomon had explored every avenue of human endeavor and pleasure open to man. He had spared no effort or expense in his search for satisfaction. His conclusion: Man's endeavors are all foolishness and futility, like chasing the wind (*see* Ecclesiastes 4:16). After musing over all the things of the world, Solomon finally concluded with the advice: "Remember your Creator in the days of your youth and keep *Him* central in your life because you will eventually face Him" (*see* Ecclesiastes 12:1). In his old age, Solomon returned to God's viewpoint and the wisdom God had given him as a young king.

Division and Bondage

Solomon's death left a weakened kingdom of Israel. Consequently, rebellion occurred and Solomon's general, Jeroboam, took ten tribes under his leadership to form the northern kingdom which continued to be called Israel. Solomon's son, Rehoboam, was able to retain only two tribes of the original twelve, both located in the southern portion of the kingdom. The two tribes were those of Judah and Benjamin and this kingdom became known as Judah. This southern area of the original kingdom, now called Judah, included Jerusalem and Solomon's Temple.

God's Spokesmen: The Prophets.   God chose to speak to His People in a different form since there no longer was a king over a unified people. Thus, from this time forward to the end of the Old Testament, God raised up prophets and spoke through them. He had used prophets before (such as Samuel during the time of Saul and David) but the importance of the prophets increased dramatically after the division of the kingdom, since God used them to call the people back to Himself and His ways.

The prophets spoke God's Word, explaining the past, exposing the sin of the present, and declaring what God was going to do in the future. They were God's appointed spokesmen, foretelling current events as well as delivering a great amount of "predictive" prophecy. Much of this predictive prophecy concerned a future, glorious Kingdom right here in God's Land. In the Garden of Eden, Eve had been given a first glimpse of the One "who would crush the head of the serpent" (*see* Genesis 3:15). Now the prophets told more about this One who would be David's Greater Son and who would rule forever on David's throne as the King of Kings.

Israel: The Northern Kingdom. Israel was the first of the two kingdoms to become engulfed in decadence and decay, brought on by the idolatry of its kings.

The northern kingdom lasted from 931 B.C. until 721 B.C. when Assyria conquered the nation and most of the inhabitants were dispersed. Even during the decadence and decay of this era, however, God never left His People without a witness. During this period of time in Israel's history a great prophet of God lived and spoke. His name was Elijah.

The message of Elijah was simple: Jehovah, *He* is God. Elijah delivered with force and power the message that God is the God of nature and the God of judgment. This was made clear when Elijah prayed for drought and got it, and when he prayed for fire from heaven and got that.

The courage of Elijah was phenomenal. He challenged everything of prominence in the northern kingdom: Ahab the king, Jezebel the queen, their power, their 850 false priests, and the people following their leadership. His challenge to the people of Israel was clear: How long will you hesitate between two opinions? If the Lord is God, follow Him; but if your idol is god, follow him.

After watching Elijah's victory over the false priests and prophets of the idol Baal, the people of Israel cried out, "Jehovah, *He* is God!" Sadly, however, the people went to their homes and nothing changed in their lives.

Elijah was a strong voice for God. The reason he could speak with such courage was that Elijah, like Moses before him, knew God personally. He also knew he was God's personal representative. That created in him the courage and the responsibility to speak out against the false gods and the hundreds of false priests and prophets arrayed against him.

The contrast between the actions of Elijah and the response of the people illustrates man's continual dilemma. The people admitted, on an intellectual basis, that Jehovah was God but they went away without establishing a personal relationship with Him. When the reality of their confrontation faded, their interest waned and their idolatrous environment again became their focus. They may even have blamed God for not being "real" to them. The fact remains that in spite of Elijah's great victory and long ministry, Israel did not turn to God and call on His name. As a result, God, true to His word, removed His protection from Israel and allowed Assyria to conquer the nation in 721 B.C., causing most of the inhabitants to be dispersed.

Judah: The Southern Kingdom.   At the very time of the fall of Israel, the southern kingdom of Judah under King Hezekiah *did* return to God and enjoyed God's protection from Assyria. But as the years passed, God's Chosen People there became more and more mechanical and less real in their worship at the Temple in Jerusalem. Worship became something they felt they had to do to appease God rather than the result of a relationship with Him by faith. This response is very common today. It is easy for us to participate in church ritual in order to be accepted by God and our fellow men. This often becomes a convenient substitute for the personal relationship God desires.

The people of Judah began to view themselves as a privileged, self-sufficient people, not dependent on God. So God sent prophets to Judah but over and over the people mocked them and rejected their message (*see* 2 Chronicles 36:15, 16). One such prophet was Isaiah. His was not an easy assignment because even before he began, God told Isaiah his mission would result in failure (*see* Isaiah 6:1–11). God said the people would neither respond nor understand and would eventually be carried into captivity by Babylon. However, God said, there would be a believing remnant through whom God's Incredible Plan would be preserved and they would eventually return to His Land.

This prophetic foretelling, two hundred years before Babylon was a great power, is miraculous and accurate in every detail. Even more amazing are the many specific details Isaiah prophesied about the coming Lamb of God. With each additional detail, the picture of God's Redemptive Plan becomes clearer as the River of God's Truth is expanding with more and more amazing facts.

Isaiah presented a far view of the One coming to rule on David's throne, to reign forevermore. On the one hand, Isaiah prophesied, He would be a normal child but on the other hand, He would be born of a virgin, truly a miracle. In addition, His name would be called:

Wonderful Counselor
Mighty God
Eternal Father
Prince of Peace

Further revelation by Isaiah pictured the One to come as a Suffering Servant who would be terribly mistreated, beaten in the face, and called the Man of Sorrows. Finally, the prophet indicated, He would be killed as a lamb led to slaughter, as a guilt offering or sacrifice for the sins of Israel and all mankind. These prophecies were not about the nation of Israel because the Suffering Servant was a Man who would suffer on behalf of Israel and its sins. By His death, He would justify, or make clean, many people (*see* Isaiah 52:14; Isaiah 53). Even Isaiah wondered what it all could mean to speak of both the Suffering Servant and His great glory afterward. The two roles did not fit together but God reassured Isaiah that the pictures were both true and would both be fulfilled in the future (*see* 1 Peter 1:10–12).

Since the kingdom of Judah was the one through which the Messiah would come, and because He was in David's line, His genealogy is carefully traced through the kings who reigned in Judah until its fall to Babylon in 586 B.C. Although some of the kings of Judah were godly servants, it was primarily the prophets who were entrusted with the specifics concerning the Messiah. Gradually, God's River of Truth (*see* Figure 4) has expanded to reveal man's condition and God's solution: "I will be your Redeemer" (*see* Isaiah 41:14; 49:7).

The prophets who delivered the message of the Messiah described Him as the Redeemer and "your King the Lord," along with many other titles. Through them, God increasingly made it clear that *He Himself* would come to Planet Earth and personally solve man's dilemma.

7

Man's System—God's Solution

At this time the world system's greatest kingdom was centered in Babylon, capital of Babylonia. This ancient area, between the Tigris and Euphrates rivers, was the same area in which the Tower of Babel was built.

The System: The Way of Man Enlarged

Mystery Babylon. Babylon was the same place where Nimrod started a political and religious system (at the Tower of Babel) as a direct challenge to God. Babylon was a kingdom of the same type as all of those ruled by Satan. Not only was Satan's purpose in Babylon to challenge God directly but it also had a more insidious purpose, represented as "Mystery Babylon."

Mystery Babylon refers to the role of Satan in veiling or masking God's Truth with a counterfeit. God reveals Truth to man and Satan continually attempts to lead man into believing something which, although it sounds like God's Truth, is a prostitution of God's revelation. Much later in the Bible, Babylon is described as the mother of those who prostitute God's Truth and promote worship of idols everywhere around the world (*see* Revelation 17:5). The counterfeit by Satan, represented by Babylon, is repeated throughout history and includes astrology, cults, and many forms of counterfeit religion. (You may want to refer back to Figure 2.) With Satan's counterfeits, he mirrors God's Word and God's plan, even to the extent of using "Christian" terminology or appearances for some of his counterfeits. Sometimes Satan finds it necessary to be extraordinarily subtle; at other points in history he can openly defy God. He uses any means necessary in his attempt to capture men's hearts for himself.

Captivity in Babylon. Babylon became the ruling power of the Middle East, just as Isaiah had prophesied more than two hundred years earlier. Babylon's ascendancy was completed by defeating Egypt in 605 B.C. After his victory, the king of Babylon, Nebuchadnezzar, besieged Jerusalem three separate times. Each time, he carried some of the Jews back to Babylon as his captives. During the last siege, which ended in 586 B.C., Nebuchadnezzar broke down the walls of Jerusalem, destroying the magnificent Temple and carrying away all of the vessels of silver and gold from the Temple.

One of the persons carried into captivity was a young teenager, a prince of Judah named Daniel. He and some other young Jewish men from the royal family were enrolled in the king's college by Nebuchadnezzar. Daniel was to be trained as a "wise man" in a curriculum which included astrology (the Babylonian religion) as well as other elements of the Chaldean culture and language (*see* Daniel 1:4, 5). During this pagan education, however, Daniel never compromised his belief in the God of Israel. His steadfast faith in God, even while being educated in the godless world system, is a wonderful example for young men and women today.

God revealed to Daniel some of the greatest prophecies in all of God's Word and commanded him to record them. The most significant prophecy concerned the mystery of the Anointed One, Messiah the Prince. Daniel's revelation was specific concerning Messiah the Prince (*see* Daniel 9:24–26), even to the point of foretelling the exact time of the presentation of Christ the King on Palm Sunday (*see* Luke 19:40–44). Daniel was entrusted with the revelation that Christ (which in Greek means "the Anointed One" or "the Messiah") was to be "cut off" or killed as the Perfect Substitute dying for the sins of imperfect man.

Return From Exile

Daniel prayed for the return of his people the Jews from the Babylonian exile. He apparently lived up to that time. After seventy years of captivity, King Cyrus issued a decree allowing the Jews who wanted to return to Jerusalem, to do so. King Cyrus stated that the Lord God of heaven had told him to issue this decree, thus fulfilling Jeremiah's prophecy (*see* Jeremiah 29:10) that the Jews would come back from Babylon "after seventy years."

Under Ezra and then Nehemiah, the Jewish remnant returned

to Judah. Under Nehemiah's leadership, the people rebuilt the walls of Jerusalem and the Temple. This Temple was not as great as Solomon's; however, it was the same Temple enlarged and beautified by King Herod, hundreds of years later.

The Closing of the Old Testament

The record of God's Incredible Plan in the Old Testament closes at this point, about 400 B.C. The next four hundred years are called the "silent years." There are sources other than the Bible, however, that indicate something of Jewish history between 400 B.C. and the birth of Christ.

The Jews were cruelly treated during much of this period and were not able to regain their status as a sovereign nation. God used these circumstances in many ways to prepare the Jews and the rest of the world for the coming of the Messiah. The timing of His arrival on Planet Earth was described by Paul as being "in the fulness of time" (*see* Galatians 4:4), and even secular history recognizes the importance of His coming in world history. Every newspaper or calendar is a testimony to the world-changing power of this One Life that was to visit Planet Earth.

People of the Book. During the period following the closing of the Old Testament, the Jews became the "people of the Book." Synagogues had been established during and after the exile and the Hebrew children were taught the Law (Torah), the Prophets, and the Psalms. God had directed the children of Israel to do this hundreds of years earlier (*see* Deuteronomy 6) but now during this period it was the rabbis (teachers) who became experts in biblical knowledge. The Jews, as a national entity, came to rely on God's Word as their guide in every area of life.

As a result of their knowledge of God's Word, the Jewish people fervently expected the Messiah. They understood the prophecies concerning His birth at Bethlehem (*see* Micah 5:2), His literal rule on David's throne (*see* Isaiah 9:6; 1 Chronicles 17:12–14), and even the approximate timetable of His coming, which was revealed by Daniel (*see* Daniel 9:24–27). When Jesus the Messiah did come, this universal knowledge of Scripture provided a base for His teaching and for the understanding of it by the people in Israel. Before their exile, the people did not know their own Scriptures but now the "fulness of time" had arrived.

Preparation for the Messiah. The rest of the world was also prepared in a unique way for the news of the Messiah to be quickly transmitted throughout the known world. Greek, one of the most exact languages ever developed, was the common language spoken and written everywhere in the Roman empire. The Jewish Scriptures (today called the Old Testament) had been translated into Greek in 250 B.C., making God's Word available to all the people. (This translation is called the Septuagint.)

The Jews rejected idolatry once and for all during this period of time and became obedient to the Scriptures. Their knowledge of Almighty God apparently was observed by some Gentiles who were tired of their useless idols and were seeking a personal God. Many had converted to Judaism and others sought to know "the Unknown God" (Acts 17:23 LB). The Jews called such Gentiles "God fearers" (*see* Acts 10) and many of these seekers could be found worshiping and learning in the synagogues where the news of the Messiah was soon to be announced. Most importantly, these synagogues and Jewish cultural centers were found not only in Jerusalem but were soon also to become strategic areas in spreading the Good News that the Messiah had come.

A final observation of this period in history discloses the fact that God had watched over the line of David in a unique way, preserving it and preparing a godly family to serve as the immediate ancestry of the Coming One. Born of a virgin (*see* Genesis 3:15; Isaiah 7:14), His name was called Jesus Christ.

The Messiah, or the Anointed One, arrived at this unique and foretold juncture in history. God's Incredible Plan had been moving inexorably toward this pivotal event for centuries. Now God's River of Truth was flowing, with an ever-increasing volume of Truth, toward Jesus Christ, who was not only to reveal Truth but who also *is* Truth.

8

Tetelestai

God's Incredible Plan is brought to its high point of fulfillment with the entry of God Himself to Planet Earth. The Bible records that "in the fulness of time, God sent His Son into the world, born of woman, born under the Law that He might redeem those who are under the Law, that they might be inheritors of His Kingdom" (*see* Galatians 4:4, 5).

Jesus' Unique Arrival

God took off His robes of glory and Sovereignty and became like us (*see* Philippians 2:7). Yet He was not exactly like us because at the same time He was 100 percent man, He was also 100 percent God. He is the Creator of the universe with the Power that holds everything together (*see* John 1:3; Hebrews 1:2; Colossians 1:17), and is the Mighty God, Eternal Father, and Prince of Peace (*see* Isaiah 9:6). Even so, He slipped into history as a helpless baby to live on Planet Earth for a time as a man.

The key to understanding the Bible is found in this one Unique Individual. Believing and knowing that Jesus Christ is Almighty God is the key to understanding God's Incredible Plan as it is revealed in both the Old and New Testaments. Perhaps even more incredible is the *way* in which God is going to solve the separation of man from God.

Jesus' Early Years. Sometime around 4 B.C., from the small Roman province of Galilee, a man named Joseph and his wife, Mary, travelled to a hamlet called Bethlehem in Judea to be enrolled in a worldwide Roman census. Joseph and Mary were descendents of David, and Bethlehem was the city of David. Mary was pregnant, even though she was a virgin.

They could not find lodgings in the town, and she gave birth to her child in a small trough for animals called a manger. In such humble surroundings God had intervened in human history in a most unusual way.

For the son she bore was not Joseph's; the child was conceived miraculously through the Holy Spirit. She was instructed by an angel to name him Jesus, which meant "Saviour." The circumstances fulfilled three of the many prophecies which the Jews applied to their expected Messiah: (1) that He would be of the line of David (*see* Isaiah 11); (2) that He would be born of a virgin and called Immanuel (God with us) (*see* Isaiah 7:14); and (3) that He would be born in Bethlehem (*see* Micah 5:2).

Other things happened that made clear the special nature of the child. Angels appeared to nearby shepherds, telling them of the birth of their Saviour, and wise men called Magi were beckoned from the East by an unusual star.

The story is familiar; we retell it every year at Christmas. The significance of the birth of Jesus is not as easily grasped, however. With His birth, God had fulfilled His promise of a Messiah Redeemer; One who would "crush the head of the serpent [Satan]" (*see* Genesis 3:15). God had come into the mire of human history as a man.

In the ensuing days, the child Jesus was miraculously recognized by Anna and Simeon, as He was presented in the Temple, and they prophesied that the promised salvation had indeed come.

Jesus the Man.   Jesus was a model son, and probably a carpenter after Joseph's trade, until, at the age of thirty, He went down to the Jordan River to be baptized by John the Baptist. The Baptist was a formidable man who wore camel skin and ate locusts and wild honey. He was considered by many a prophet, Israel's first in some four or five centuries, and he stirred up considerable excitement among the common people, many of whom responded to his call for repentance.

He was also fearless, speaking out against those of the religious and political authorities who were wicked men and declaring God's impending judgment on them. Some of the people even considered him the Messiah, but he denied it, quoting Isaiah to define his mission:

[I am] the voice of one crying in the wilderness, Prepare a
road for the Lord.

See Matthew 3:3

He did say that One was coming after him, One whose sandal he
was not fit to untie.

When Jesus went down to be baptized, it was to identify with
John the Baptist and reveal to him that Jesus was that "One."
John baptized Jesus only at His insistence, and as He was baptized, John saw the Spirit of God descend on Him as a dove. At
that moment, a voice came from heaven, saying, "This is My
beloved Son, in whom I am well-pleased" (Matthew 3:17).
With the descent of the Spirit, John recognized Jesus as the Messiah Redeemer and later said, "Behold the Lamb of God, who
takes away the sin of the world" (*see* John 1:36).

Jesus, having received the testimony of His Father, was now
ready to begin His ministry. But first He was led into the Judean
wilderness where He fasted and prayed in preparation for His
public ministry. After forty days of fasting Satan came to the
weakened and hungry Jesus and tried to coax Him into sin. Satan
tried to get Jesus to abuse His special status by suggesting that He
turn the desert stones into bread, and Jesus, despite His hunger,
replied, "Man shall not live by bread alone, but on every word
that comes from the mouth of God." Satan, rebuffed, then asked
Him to throw Himself off the Temple, saying that angels would
come and arrest His fall. Jesus refused again, and said,
"You shall not tempt the Lord." Then Satan in this ultimate
temptation offered Jesus all the kingdoms of the world which
were his to give if only Jesus would bow down and worship him.
Jesus refused once more, replying, "You shall worship the Lord
God, and Him alone." Satan then left, utterly defeated (*see* Luke
4:1–13).

By refusing the temptations of Satan, Jesus, though fully human, proved Himself to be quite different from Adam, who fell.
Whereas Adam and Eve chose not to believe God's Word, Jesus
did obey, although His only resource was the Spirit. He was in a
position no different from the one Adam was in, yet He proved to
be without sin.

As the "Last Adam," He had thwarted Satan, and now He was ready to attack Satan's world, the mirror kingdom. Jesus is called the Last Adam because He lived as Adam was created to live, as a man containing the very Life of God (*see* 1 Corinthians 15:45).

The Kingdom of God

Jesus the Messiah began His work in Galilee, announcing His mission in words very similar to those of John the Baptist: "The time has come! The kingdom of God is at hand! Believe the Good News" (*see* Mark 1:27).

In His hometown of Nazareth He was even more direct; when He went up to speak at the synagogue, He quoted from a messianic promise in Isaiah:

> The Spirit of the Lord is upon me; he has appointed me to preach Good News to the poor; he has sent me to heal the brokenhearted and to announce that captives shall be released and the blind shall see, that the downtrodden shall be freed from their oppressors, and that God is ready to give blessings to all who come to him.
>
> Luke 4:18, 19 LB

He sat down and then said, "These Scriptures came true today!" (Luke 4:21 LB). The people of Nazareth were amazed, and although they rejected Him as their Messiah, word spread all around Galilee and the neighboring provinces.

Powerful Proofs. Jesus, having already surprised the people with His claim of being the Messiah, showed them His extraordinary Power. As Jesus and His disciples travelled from town to town in Judea and Galilee, He performed nature miracles, healing miracles, and controlled the spirit world. On several occasions He performed the unheard-of miracle of raising people from the dead. Because Jesus Christ is God He had the Power to suspend the laws of nature for His purposes. God has always used miracles as announcements that He is redeeming man, just as He did when He brought out the Israelites from Egypt. God verifies His Almighty Power by miracles, for we cannot perceive His

Power simply with our five senses. So it was when He came to earth as the Messiah Redeemer.

Here is a dramatic sequence in which Jesus proved His Power as God. First He showed His control of nature when He calmed the storm on the Sea of Galilee with just a word (*see* Mark 4:37–41). Next Christ demonstrated His Power over the spirit world as He cast legions of them out of a man even while the evil spirits were recognizing Him as "Jesus, Son of the Most High God" (Mark 5:8 LB). Then a synagogue official named Jairus asked Jesus to heal his sick daughter. They were on the way to his home when a sick woman came up behind Him in the crowd and touched His cloak. Immediately she was healed and instantly Jesus knew He had healed her by His Power, so He asked whoever had touched Him to come forward. In the pressing crowd of people His disciples said, "You see the multitudes pressing in on You and You say, 'Who touched Me?'" (*see* Mark 5:31). This illustrated ever more graphically His supernatural nature. After the woman came forward and admitted her healing, Jesus commended her act of faith, sending her home completely healed. By this time the sick little girl had died. At Jairus's home everyone was distraught and crying. Jesus told them not to fear but to believe. Then He gently took her by the hand and raised her from the dead. The question arises: Who but God can raise a person from the dead? Everyone there was completely astounded (*see* Mark 5:42). By this significant progression of miracles on one day Jesus proved who He *is* by what He did—first as Lord over nature, then the spirit world, then disease, and finally man's greatest enemy, death.

Nor was this all. Another dramatic way in which Jesus proved His deity was the healing of a paralytic man. Before healing the man Jesus said, "Your sins are forgiven you" (*see* Matthew 9:2). The watching Pharisees knew that only God, our Creator, has the right to forgive sins. The healing of the paralytic man was of secondary importance to anyone who really understood the situation; but by healing the man, Jesus gave additional proof of His right to forgive sins. By publicly forgiving sin, Jesus was making a positive declaration to the people that He was God.

Soon the people sought Him so much that He found it difficult

to enter their towns, and usually remained out in the countryside
with His disciples, where the people came to Him by the hundreds.

The Miracles and the Kingdom.   At this point, we might ask
some questions: What was the significance of what He was doing?
What did He mean by the Kingdom of God? The two questions
are tied up with each other, and we will answer the last one first.

By the Kingdom of God He meant God's gracious rule, the
loving Power that effected these healings and ordered out the
demonic spirits. In the Person of Jesus, God's Power and Love
had come, ripping apart the bonds imposed on man by Satan, and
He was on earth to comfort the people long oppressed.

The Kingdom of God was present where Jesus was present; it
had come with Him and He was the long-awaited Messiah. Although the completion of His mission awaited Him in His death,
for the time being He was Israel's Messiah, fulfilling the prophecy
from Isaiah which He had read at Nazareth.

Jesus Himself saw the significance of His work this way. When
disciples of John the Baptist came (the Baptist was in prison),
they brought a question: "Are you really the one we are waiting
for, or shall we keep on looking?" Jesus replied, "Go back to
John and tell him about the miracles you've seen me do—the
blind people I've healed, and the lame people now walking without help, and the cured lepers, and the deaf who hear, and the
dead raised to life; and tell him about my preaching the Good
News to the poor. Then give him this message, 'Blessed are those
who don't doubt me' " (Matthew 11:3–6 LB). He based His claim
to be the coming Messiah on the gracious and miraculous works
He was performing.

Jesus also based His claim to be the Agent of the Kingdom of
God on His Power over the demonic forces. When the Pharisees
accused Him of driving out demons by the power of Satan, He
showed them how absurd it was to think that Satan would be
aligned against himself. Then He said, "If I drive out demons by
the Spirit of God, then the Kingdom of God is upon you" (*see*
Matthew 12:28).

The Teaching of Jesus—He Redefines the Mosaic Law

Jesus not only showed the people the Power of the Kingdom of God but He taught them about it as well: what it was like, how one could enter it, and its ethical standards.

In the Sermon on the Mount, Jesus taught the people what righteousness was and what God's Righteousness was. He sharpened and superceded the Law Moses had given them. He could only do this because He was God in human form.

The key phrases Jesus used to clarify the Law were, "The Law of Moses said . . . but I say . . . ." This demonstrated that His authority was greater than that of Moses. In the sermon, Jesus pointed to the fact that God sees and judges the inner motives and thoughts of men. Whereas Moses had commanded them not to murder, Jesus told them not to hate or have ill feelings in their hearts toward another person. And whereas Moses had commanded them not to commit adultery, Jesus told them that desire for someone they were not married to was enough of a sin to send them to hell. Furthermore He warned them against outward righteousness, or showing off their righteousness as the Pharisees did, "praying on the streetcorner so that men might notice them, and giving their money offerings to a flourish of trumpets" (*see* Matthew 5, 6). Instead of doing these things to get attention, Jesus said, one should do them before the Father, in private. "Blessed are the pure in heart," He said, "for they shall see God" (Matthew 5:8).

The most startling requirement to enter the Kingdom of God, said Jesus, is that *we* "are to be perfect, even as God in heaven is perfect" (*see* Matthew 5:48). In other words, the Sermon on the Mount is God's Value System *internalized* and it has no loopholes for "rationalizing" our sins.

Having commanded this, having asked us to forgive all men, even to love our enemies, did Jesus really expect anyone to live up to His standards? Could any mere mortal, with all his effort, live in such a way?

No. Only God is good, and only God could give this righteousness. This is why Jesus made the profound claim that He came to fulfill the *intent* of the Mosaic Law. By this, He claimed that He was meeting God's requirements on our behalf, excusing us from this responsibility (*see* Romans 10:4). And herein lies the answer to our first question: The significance of what Christ came to do is that He is our Substitute. He fulfilled the Law, which we cannot do, and died in our place so that we need not die. Only God could perform this miracle, and this is the wonderful transaction Jesus came to make for us, as we will see.

The Conflict With the Pharisees

The Pharisees, on the whole, were unhappy with the teaching of Jesus, and many of them actively opposed Him. Some were open to His message, and it is reasonable to assume that some of them found faith. Many of them admired Jesus at first, and would from time to time invite Him to dinner. They called Him "Rabbi" which indicates the respect they had for Him.

But the message He spoke was hard medicine for them. The Pharisees were a fanatical and pious group of Jews who were held in high esteem, even awe, by the common people, for their strict adherence to the Law and the "traditions of the elders." The Pharisees, however, did not much esteem the common people. In fact, they held the common people in contempt as lowly sinners, ignorant and unworthy. And for the most part, the Pharisees, proud as they were, did not see fit to associate with "sinners."

Jesus thought differently. Compassion was the key to His ministry, and He dined often with tax collectors, prostitutes, and common people: the "sinners," many of whom repented and were forgiven. "It is not the healthy who need a doctor, but the sick . . . . I have come not to call the righteous, but to call sinners" (*see* Matthew 9:12, 13).

Not that Jesus considered any of the Pharisees "righteous." He had told the crowd at the Sermon on the Mount that "unless your righteousness surpasses that of the scribes and the Pharisees you will certainly not enter the Kingdom of heaven" (*see* Matthew 5:20). Jesus' criterion for righteousness (and the Father's as well) was that if a man was guilty of one infraction, he was guilty of all (*see* James 2:10).

The problem with the Pharisees was that they *thought* they were righteous and felt no need to repent. This is instructive for us. Irregardless of our presumed virtue, no accumulation of good and noble deeds makes us worthy to come into God's presence.

And What About Their Religious Traditions? Jesus taught with authority and kept scraping away their man-made religious traditions in order to get down to God's original intention: to have a personal relationship with man. Needless to say, this irked the Pharisees, who were confirmed traditionalists. They were also notorious externalists with their traditions. To be seen of men was their religious activity. They had numerous complaints against Jesus and His disciples, for instance, that they did not obey the many traditions about how to observe the Sabbath. But Jesus said that the Sabbath was made for man, not man for the Sabbath. He once confounded the Pharisees by asking them, as they stood around disapproving a healing He was performing on the Sabbath, whether it was right to do good or evil on the Sabbath. There was nothing they could say. Jesus often accused the Pharisees of teaching their man-made laws instead of those from God; of being content with their ritualistic outward religion rather than being *in*wardly pure. *Very often the "religious" person depends on ritual and tradition for Eternal Life, because God's basic Truth is so cloaked with tradition that its real meaning is hidden to the worshiper.*

Jesus' conflict with the unbelieving religious leaders increased in intensity until they began conspiring together to kill Him. He was directly challenging their power.

The Identity of Jesus

Having established one source of conflict between Jesus and the Pharisees, concerning how a man is justified before God, we turn now to another: the identity of Jesus.

Through all of His ministry Jesus claimed to be the Messiah, to be divine and coeternal with God. He had numerous arguments with the Pharisees on this matter.

Most of them did not believe He was divine despite His manifest Righteousness and many miraculous acts. Jesus asked them, if they were unwilling to accept His testimony, to believe on His works, but they were unwilling to do even that. He told them if they did not believe Him they were not believing in the

Father who had sent Him, for He was the revelation of the Father.

He claimed to be coeternal with God (*see* John 8:58), calling Himself Yahweh as He had to Moses hundreds of years earlier, and of the same essence as the Father (*see* John 10:30). On both occasions the Jews understood Him well enough to pick up stones to stone Him for blasphemy. It was this, along with His claim to be Messiah and His actions in the Temple (He cleared the Temple of its merchants, not willing to let His Father's house be a "den of thieves"), [Mark 11:17] that made them decide to murder Him.

It is worth noting that if Jesus was *not* God, He must have been lying or out of His mind. And such a man would not have been able to teach great principles of Truth if He were unbalanced or disposed to lying.

The Pharisees charged Jesus with blaspheming God, and Jesus charged them with blaspheming Him and the Father. He said, "You dishonor both Me and My Father who sent Me" (*see* John 8:49).

Jesus is God.   The wonderful part about God coming into the world, coming right down where we are, is that it shows His great Love for everyone. It was God who took the initiative. It was *His* idea to become a man, step into history, and communicate this Love to us. Jesus communicated this compassionate Love and acceptance to everyone He met—and thousands of people responded to Him immediately.

He reached all kinds of people from the rich to the poor, involving Himself in their lives, performing miracles of all kinds, and teaching them with many different methods.

Vast crowds followed Jesus everywhere He travelled. People of all kinds responded to His invitation, "Come unto me . . . and you shall find rest for your souls" (*see* Matthew 11:28, 29). He explained simply and clearly how each person could relate to Him as God. His concepts were down to earth with phrases such as "I am the bread of life . . ." (John 6:35), "I came to give you Eternal Life" (*see* John 10:28), and "I am the Way, the Truth, and the Life, and no man comes to God but through Me" (*see* John 14:6).

But His most illuminating words were spoken to Nicodemus, a

Pharisee and a member of the Sanhedrin, the Jewish ruling council. Nicodemus knew that Jesus could not perform such miracles without God's Power, and therefore he considered Jesus a virtual prophet. He came to Jesus one night secretly (probably so that his peers on the Sanhedrin would not find out) and Jesus told him that he must be "born again" (born from above) or he would not see the Kingdom of God. When Nicodemus asked incredulously, or sarcastically, how a man could reenter his mother's womb, Jesus said that one must be born of the Spirit to enter the Kingdom. Nicodemus was still baffled, so Jesus explained further. Our first birth is of the flesh, our human birth. But to be in God's Kingdom, every person must be spiritually alive—born again by the Spirit of God (*see* John 3:7). (That third dimension, our spirit, died as a result of Adam and Eve's choice, as we saw in chapter 3, and has to be brought back to life in order to have Eternal Life.) Concluding their conversation, Jesus told Nicodemus that He must be sacrificed so that men could have Everlasting Life. He had come to save, not to condemn. His mission is stated in the simple and beautiful words, "For God loved the world so much that he gave his only Son so that anyone who believes in him shall not perish but have eternal life" (John 3:16 LB).

Jesus and the Disciples

As we have seen, Jesus came to the people of Israel as their long-awaited Messiah, healing their sick, giving sight to the blind, even raising the dead. He poured out His Love and His Life for them, visiting their homes and befriending them. But the religious leaders were aligned against Him, and the other people were fickle. Jesus saw that Israel would reject Him.

Jesus then, forseeing His own death at the hands of the Jewish religious leaders, intensified His work with His disciples. These disciples were twelve men who lived with Him, watched Him heal the sick and control nature itself, men who gradually learned who He really was as they watched Him and heard Him teach.

What sort of men were the disciples? They were ordinary, fallible men; some were formerly fishermen, one had been a tax gatherer, another had been a political subversive. Peter, James, and John, the three who appear to have been closest to Jesus, were all quite impulsive.

It was Jesus' unconditional Love which drew these men ever closer to Him. He met them where they were, accepting them completely, living with them and serving them. As they walked together and ate together Jesus taught them, often by parable, what it meant to be a member of the Kingdom of God. His definition of the Kingdom was much different from the ideas they had been taught before, and they had a difficult time adjusting themselves to it. Their Messiah-King insisted that His Kingdom started very small, like a tiny seed, within a person's heart. It grew secretly until "first a leaf-blade pushed through, and later the wheat-heads formed and finally the grain ripened" (Mark 4:28 LB). The growth depended on the soil, which in Jesus' parable stood for the heart. The parable illustrated a consistent spiritual truth: God will work in any willing heart.

Jesus sent the disciples out to preach the Good News throughout the surrounding area, investing His spiritual authority in them. This was the method He used as a test, to see if the Truth He was teaching them was entering their hearts and changing their lives. However, He was not concerned about their failures, only their lack of faith. He knew if they believed in Him He could change them, so He just asked them to put their faith in Him. Some miracles were performed largely for their benefit, such as the feeding of the five thousand (it was also a humane act) and some were performed *solely* for their benefit, for example, when He walked on the water or when He calmed a storm which blew up while they were out on the lake. The latter miracle made them all wonder who He was, that even storms obeyed Him.

Having spent much time with them, He finally asked them who they thought He was. The disciples were timid, afraid to answer. Peter then spoke up, and said, "The Christ, the Messiah, the Son of the living God." Jesus told him, "God has blessed you, Simon, son of Jonah, for my Father in heaven has personally revealed this to you—this is not from any human source" (Matthew 16:16, 17 LB). Jesus commended Peter's response to God's revelation, even though Peter obviously didn't yet understand the significance of the Messiah, or His purpose on Planet Earth.

As Jesus was training His disciples, He used every opportunity to prepare them for His death and Resurrection. Repeatedly He taught that He came into the world to offer Himself as the Perfect and Last Sacrifice for sins. "I, the Messiah, am not here to be served, but to help others, and to give my life as a ransom for many" (Mark 10:45 LB). And how would this come about? "From then on Jesus began to speak plainly to his disciples about going to Jerusalem, and what would happen to him there—that he would suffer at the hands of the Jewish leaders, that he would be killed, and that three days later he would be raised to life again" (Matthew 16:21 LB). This upset the disciples, particularly Peter, but Jesus bluntly told them it was necessary for Him to die—to conquer death and sin.

The Problem of Death

Man created a problem resulting in death and separation from God. This problem was observed in the Garden of Eden when Adam and Eve chose against God. (*See* Figure 3 earlier in the book.) Because the character of God includes all of His attributes, God could not pour out His **Love** at the expense of His **Sovereignty**. Adam had challenged God's **Sovereignty** when he challenged God's right to rule. This self-rule was sin and could not be allowed in God's presence because of His **Righteousness** and **Holiness**. God had to pronounce the sentence of death on Adam in order to deal **Justly** with him. Since God is **Immutable** (unchangeable), the sentence of death He imposed has been carried out.

God's solution to the problem of the slavery of death is the most wonderful expression of His **Wisdom** (Omniscience) and **Power** (Omnipotence) in all of history. The solution makes it possible for God to pour out His Love upon all mankind, from Adam to the end of time (*see* Hebrews 2:14, 15).

The King Is Publicly Presented

Jesus worked perhaps His greatest miracle before going to Jerusalem when He raised His friend Lazarus from the dead. Lazarus had been in the tomb three days while his family and the

people of his community mourned, and when Jesus brought Him
back to life, the word spread like fire. But the reaction of the
unbelieving Pharisees was not belief in Jesus as their Messiah
even in the face of this incontrovertible proof. Instead they completed their plot to kill Him. Such is the *blindness of unbelief!*

Shortly after that, Jesus travelled to Jerusalem for the last time.
His disciples procured Him a donkey, and He rode into Jerusalem
on the donkey in accordance with the prophecy in Zechariah:
"Behold, your king comes to you, gentle and riding on a donkey"
(*see* Zechariah 9:9). By doing this, Jesus was making an open,
public claim to be the Messiah. The crowd, swelled by the many
pilgrims visiting Jerusalem for the Passover, laid a path of palm
branches out before Him and shouted, "Hosanna to the Son of
David! Blessed is He who comes in the name of the Lord!" The
Pharisees asked Him to rebuke His disciples and the crowd, but
Jesus replied, "I tell you, if they keep quiet the stones will cry
out!" (*see* Luke 19:40).

Jesus then wept over Jerusalem as He approached it, prophesy-
ing its destruction (it was destroyed by Roman armies in 63 and
then A.D. 70) and saying, "They [the Jews' enemies] will not
leave one stone on another, because you did not recognize the
time of God's coming to you" (*see* Luke 19:44). The Romans
fulfilled this prophecy explicitly. They had heard that there was
gold hidden between the stones so they dismantled every stone of
the magnificent Temple.

Passover

Jesus spent His last evening with His disciples celebrating the
Passover meal. The Passover was the ceremony God had given
His people portraying His Redemptive Plan. And although the
Jewish people obediently ate the Passover meal year after year as
God had ordained, little did they know (until this night) what the
symbolism really meant. It was at this last Passover meal that
Jesus revealed what the symbolism had foreshadowed all those
centuries. The traditional wine represented His blood, and the
bread was His broken body. Together they symbolize the work of
atonement accomplished by Christ on the cross, and our need to
personally receive it. Today Communion is an extension of the

old Jewish Passover because both point to God's redemptive work here on Planet Earth.

The Centrality of the Cross

God provided this wonderful solution for man's separation from Him, and central to God's Redemptive Plan is the cross.

The sacrifice of Jesus on the cross makes it possible for any person to be lifted out of the bondage of the world system into which he is born. The Bible describes this: "He lifted me up out of the pit of destruction . . . and set my feet upon a rock" (*see* Psalms 40:2). Throughout His ministry, Christ told His followers that the reason He came to earth was to die for the remission (taking away) of sins. With absolute clarity about His mission on earth, Christ said that He was voluntarily laying down His Life and no man would take it from Him. He also said that He would take up His Life again (*see* John 10:17, 18).

Arrest and Trial.   Jesus was arrested that Passover night by the Jewish religious leaders and brought before their high priest for trial. During His trial the only charge which could be made against Jesus is very significant: it was blasphemy, meaning that He claimed to be God. No doubt should exist about who Jesus claimed to be. The only question we have to answer for ourselves is whether or not we believe Him. There is no middle ground; either **He is a liar and an egomaniac or He is Jehovah God as He claims to be.** The high priest did not believe Jesus was the Messiah and God so he condemned Him to death for blasphemy. Pilate, the Roman ruler, finally gave official permission for Christ's Crucifixion, although he himself could find no guilt in Him (*see* John 18:38).

Tetelestai!   It is not within the scope of this book to detail all of the Life of Jesus the Messiah, but rather to focus upon the *reason* He came and the *work of God's Love* which He accomplished on the cross. As He hung on that barbarous cross offering up His Life as the Last and Perfect Sacrifice, His utterances demonstrated the eternal transaction being made.

The most poignant cry of Christ pictured His estrangement

from His own Essence as God: "My God, my God, why have you forsaken me?" (Matthew 27:46 LB). Darkness was over the whole land, even though it was the middle of the day, symbolizing what Christ was suffering: *all* the sins of *all* mankind of *all* time—past, present, and future—were placed on Him. At that instant, Jesus, the Holy One of Israel, became **Sin** (*see* 2 Corinthians 5:21). In an act of incomparable **Love,** Jesus took upon Himself our sins so that we need not die! As a consequence of becoming sin, God the Father could not fellowship with Him. Thus, the cry of agony and horror from Jesus.

The last word spoken by Jesus as He hung on the cross was entirely different and in sharp contrast to His preceding words. The last word spoken was *Tetelestai* and it was a cry of victory (*see* Colossians 2:14). *Tetelestai* is a Greek word which means "paid in full." In the Roman world a convicted criminal and his crimes were listed on a so-called certificate of debt. After the criminal had served his sentence for the crimes, this same word *Tetelestai* was written across the certificate meaning "this matter is finished" or "paid in full." It is in this sense of "paid in full" that Jesus cried it out on the cross. Christ "paid in full" for every sin held against every person by the **Just** Judge of all mankind, God Himself.

If all our sins are paid for, if all God's wrath has been poured out on Christ, then all that condemnation has been taken by Him and there is none left for us. If there had been *one* sin left unpaid in the past, present, or future, the Messiah of all mankind could not have risen from the dead. When He did rise from the dead, three days later, it was God the Father saying, "Amen—My wrath is propitiated." That is why *propitiation* is one of the greatest love words in the Bible: it means "God is satisfied" (*see* 1 John 4:10).

The moment Jesus died as the Unblemished Sacrifice, the heavy woven veil in the Temple, leading into the Holy of Holies, was torn from top to bottom (*see* Matthew 27:51). The tearing of the veil was God's declaration that man could now approach Him in person. No longer was it necessary to have the high priest sprinkle blood on the mercy seat once a year.

Jesus Is the Last High Priest.   ''Now we may walk right into the very Holy of Holies where God is, because of the blood of Jesus. This is the . . . life-giving way which Christ has opened up for us by tearing the curtain—his human body—to let us into the holy presence of God'' (Hebrews 10:19, 20 LB).

Resurrection and Ascension.   Jesus died on the cross but three days later, unlike any other religious leader, He rose miraculously from the dead just as He had told His followers He would (*see* John 2:19). He was seen by many people repeatedly for forty days. He proved His literal physical bodily Resurrection over and over by eating with His followers and inviting them to touch Him so they would know He was not just a spirit. He also taught them about Himself from their own Scriptures, showing how He had fulfilled all the Old Testament prophecies (*see* Luke 24; John 20).

Christ then literally ascended from the Mount of Olives. Two angels assured the astonished disciples that Jesus would return someday in precisely the same way He ascended: literally and bodily (*see* Acts 1:9–11).

These two miraculous events, His Resurrection and Ascension, climaxed God's visit to Planet Earth. Jesus told His disciples that He would leave them, but He would send the Comforter, the Holy Spirit, who would Himself empower them to start and carry out Christ's commission on earth.

The meaning of Christ's Resurrection for you and for me is the same as for the Apostle Paul. Paul stated that Christ's Resurrection is the proven assurance (*see* Acts 17:31) to us that he **is God** and that He has conquered the slavery of death forever (*see* Hebrews 2:14, 15). It is clear that the observers closest to the situation knew that Christ's Resurrection was not an illusion, not symbolic, nothing other than a miraculous and physical Resurrection from death. Paul even stated that if it is not a true fact then we Christians are of all men most to be pitied: our faith is worthless and we are still in our sins (*see* 1 Corinthians 15:17–19). It is clear that this triumph is *central* to the forgiveness of our sins and our hope for Eternal Life with our Lord, Jesus Christ.

A Summary of God's Logic of Love

The previous pages have described the important events of God's Redemptive Plan. These events reveal God's Logic of Love and His decision to become what we are, human form, in order that He could bear the consequences of His own judgment on our sins.

Because of the centrality of redemption in understanding God's Incredible Plan, the essentials of God's Logic of Love are summarized below:

1. The Judge of the universe proclaimed the sentence of death, both spiritual and physical, on all men. "All men have sinned . . . . The wages of sin is death" (*see* Romans 3:23; 6:23).
2. After the sentence, the Judge took off His robes of glory and majesty, became the defendant, and took that sentence of death on Himself. "Christ became sin that we might be the righteousness of God" (*see* 2 Corinthians 5:21). ". . . only as a human being could he die and in dying break the power of the devil who had the power of death" (Hebrews 2:14 LB).
3. God stood in man's place, bearing the divine wrath for all people's sins, for all time. Bridging the separation, "Christ Jesus took the punishment for our sins . . . Christ's blood and our faith is the means of saving us from His wrath" (*see* Romans 3:25).
4. This act of **Love** by God is called *propitiation,* meaning to satisfy the demands of a Righteous and Just God. "In this is love, not that we loved God, but that He loved us, and sent His Son to be the propitiation for our sins" (1 John 4:10). "He is the one who took God's wrath against our sins upon himself, and brought us into fellowship with God; and he is the forgiveness for our sins . . ." (1 John 2:2 LB).

The cross was necessary because there was no other way that reconciliation could be made in order that man could be brought back to God (*see* Acts 4:12). In this way God set Himself free to love man without sacrificing any of His attributes. (*See* Figure 3 earlier in the book.) His Sovereignty is vindicated.

The centrality of Christ's death on the cross in God's Redemptive Plan for us as individuals is indicated because:

1. The cross of Christ is the *only* ground upon which man can approach God.
2. The cross of Christ is the proof of God's rejection of *all* human merit, self-righteousness, or self-effort.

If God were to forgive or accept even one person on the basis of good works, sincerity, trying hard, or religious activity, then the cross of Christ would be either God's greatest folly or the greatest crime in history.

A Concluding Perspective

God did not make any mistake, nor was Christ's death on the cross an accident. "He is the Lamb of God sacrificed before the foundation of the world" (*see* Revelation 13:8). Jesus rose from the dead, literally and bodily, and in so doing, He conquered death for each person who accepts Him (*see* Hebrews 2:14–17).

Now God's only issue with all people in the world is this: Will you accept the gift of Eternal Life? Will you receive His forgiveness? Are you willing to contain God's Eternal Life? "For God so loved the world that He gave His only begotten Son, that whoever believes in Him should not perish, but have Eternal Life" (*see* John 3:16).

9

The Body of Christ—The Church

The Redemptive Plan for dealing with the separation of man from God has been completed, as described in the previous chapter. The next significant stage of God's Kingdom is the church.

As we have seen, *Jehovah God* has dealt with man's separation when He came in the Person of *Jesus the Messiah*. His once-for-all sacrifice makes it possible for *God the Holy Spirit* to at last personally indwell man's spirit (*see* John 7:39). Using the analogy of the glove (described in the third chapter of this book), man is created like a glove, to contain God's divine Life. It is God the Holy Spirit who, like the hand, fills the "glove" of man with God's Eternal Life.

The Holy Spirit

The birth of the church occurred when the Holy Spirit came to dwell in a group of individuals, transforming them into dynamic men and women who turned the world upside down (*see* Acts 17:6). To understand the church and its growth, therefore, it is necessary to consider in more detail the Person of the Holy Spirit.

The Holy Spirit was the One who was "moving over the face of the waters" in creation (*see* Genesis 1:2). He is always the One who strives with man, convincing him of his sinful condition and bringing him to repentance (*see* John 16:8). In a word, the Holy Spirit is the Agent who initiates a personal relationship between the Creator and created, by dwelling in the *spirit* of man. We must have the Holy Spirit to know and worship God, for as Jesus said, "God is a Spirit, and man must have His help to worship Him (*see* John 4:24).

The Holy Spirit does not assume bodily form but this in no way prevents Him from being a real Person. He is *not* just a force or powerful influence. We should have no difficulty in understanding this concept, since we are all aware that our own physical body is just a "clay pot" or "house" containing the real person, which is our unseen but expressed personality. Our personality (soul) is tied inseparably with our immortal spirit continuing on eternally, after physical death. The Holy Spirit is the One who is able to bring our human spirit to life. He brings in Eternal Life, replacing the eternal death with which we are born. This is what Jesus called the "new birth," and everyone needs it. This "new birth" occurs when an individual believes in Christ and accepts Him as Lord and God.

The Birth of the Church

The Holy Spirit came after Christ's bodily Ascension and gave birth to the church (*see* John 16:7), making Christ's Eternal Life available to everyone. The specific day the Holy Spirit came and the church was born is called Pentecost.

The church is people—people who contain Jesus' divine Life within them. Corporately, these people are called the Body of Christ, with Christ Himself as the Head (*see* Ephesians 1:22, 23). Their spiritual union with Christ and with each other is far beyond any human relationship. In the Body of Christ, the relationship is both vertical and horizontal. It is vertical in the sense that all its members are related personally to God in a supernatural way, sharing His divine nature through the Holy Spirit (*see* 2 Peter 1:4). The relationship is horizontal with fellowship among the members based upon a union of love which parallels the Love and communion in the three Persons of the Godhead (*see* John 17:11, 21).

The Kingdom of God Within Man. Jesus taught His disciples that the church is the "Kingdom of God within you" (*see* Luke 17:21), but He did not mean a kingdom of earthly power and splendor. Rather, Jesus taught that this Kingdom was people expressing God's Life within the world system—a Life which is like salt flavoring a bowl of soup.

Life within this Kingdom finds both inward and outward expression in love. Before He left, Jesus gave a new command, namely, that His followers are to love exactly as He loves (*see* John 13:34, 35). Obviously, the only possible way man can express this kind of love is to *contain the divine Life of Christ*. God's Love is unconditional and sacrificial because He loves people just as they are and He keeps on loving them even when they do not respond to His Love. A love such as that is life changing. It is a dynamic force more revolutionary than the mightiest army of any kingdom in the whole world system.

It is now clear how we can live as the mediators of God's Kingdom on earth. This is only possible because of what God does through us, and not what we, in our own human power, are capable of doing. God's Life can be expressed, His Power demonstrated, and His Light made to shine through us, even while Satan's kingdom is in full operation on Planet Earth.

The Function of the Church

The function of the church is very simple. It was expressed by Jesus to His followers, just before He ascended, when He told them to take the Good News to all the world. The Good News to which He referred was the message to people that God has paid for their sins and offers to them a love relationship with Himself. This Gospel is the best news that anyone could hear! It is so wonderful to discover that in spite of all our wrongdoing, God loves each of us individually and unconditionally and has made it possible for us to have a personal relationship with Him, the Creator-God of the universe.

When we accept Christ as Lord, asking Him into our hearts, we become members of His Body, the church. The function of the Body of Christ, therefore, is to offer Life, God's Eternal Life, to every person. The controversy in the universe between Satan and God is over *Life* and *death*. Satan's approach to Eve in the Garden of Eden resulted in death from that day on, meaning spiritual death or alienation from God. The fundamental problem of man, then, is not good versus evil but rather Eternal Life versus eternal death. The Gospel message to be spread by the church is that death can be replaced by Eternal Life. The function of the church is the offering of this Eternal Life to all the people of the world in every age.

Every person who has Christ in him (the meaning of the word *Christian*) is to become an ambassador for Christ, reconciling the world to God (*see* 2 Corinthians 5:17–21). The Early Church did just that, and it multiplied rapidly throughout the Roman Empire and even beyond. Within thirty years the church numbered in the millions.

The Malfunction of the Church

Sadly, in the succeeding centuries the church has often been infiltrated by the world system. Why does this happen? Jesus taught His disciples, in parables, about the sequence of the church age and what they should expect. In the first parable, the Good News is like good seed sown on different kinds of soil such as the hard soil, the rocky soil, among thorns, and finally on the good soil. The soil represents different responses to Christ and His church (the seed), depending on the receptivity of a man's heart, as the Holy Spirit reveals Christ to him.

The logical reaction to the amazing growth of the Early Church was for the master counterfeiter, Satan himself, to infiltrate and undermine God's Kingdom from within. Christ described this strategy in another parable about His wheat field, which represented the Body of Believers. Christ warned that His enemy, Satan, would secretly sow tares in His wheat field at night. Tares are weeds which *look like* wheat, grow up with the wheat in the field, but, of course, do not bear the crop which the farmer wants to harvest. However, he does not remove the tares out of his field until the harvest. They *both* grow side by side, until the end, when only the wheat is saved.

The counterfeit sowing is within the church. There are seven "representative" churches, which actually existed in the first century, and they are described in letters from Christ in Revelation 2 and 3. They were apparently chosen for their distinct characteristics which occur in churches throughout the church age. These messages reveal the subtle ways in which Satan infiltrates the church, cutting away the essential truths of God's Word a little at a time. Gradually, the church becomes an organization built largely on men's traditions and finally results in what is described as an "apostate" church. Apostasy means "a defection from the truth."

The apostate church is a mirror image of God's church. It looks the same but is backwards (*refer* back to Figure 2). Satan accomplishes apostasy by a subtle undermining of God's Word, by distorted teaching about the church, and by leaving out essential truths concerning Christ's work on the cross. The most insidious aspect of this strategy is the attempt of Satan to distort the character of God Himself in the Persons of Christ and the Holy Spirit. Throughout the church age, the deity of Christ and His finished work on the cross has been the focal point of Satan's hatred and attack. Countless distortions of God's Truth resulted down through the years since the intent of God's adversary is continually to deceive God's people and derail God's plan for man's redemption.

But the true church, which is the Body of Christ, has always been preserved, and Christ promised that even the gates of hell would not be able to overthrow His Kingdom (*see* Matthew 16:18). As in the Old Testament, true believers are "God's remnant," and they are always present in the church.

Apostate Apathy.   The last great apostate expression of the church age is known as the Laodicean church, and contains within it *all* of the world system.

This Laodicean church is the perfect counterfeit, Satan's masterpiece, the result of his strategy to mirror God's Kingdom. It is not surprising that Satan infiltrates the church, masquerading as an "angel of light" and placing *un*believers in key positions as "ministers of righteousness" (2 Corinthians 11:14, 15). Satan has no quarrel with "religion." Religion helps to accomplish Satan's highest goal: worship of *himself* in place of God (*see* 2 Thessalonians 2:11; 2 Timothy 3:2-5).

Overt warfare. The warfare on Planet Earth between God's people and Satan's forces is sometimes *overt* (i.e., visible and obvious). An example of Satan's overt strategy is the often obvious way Satan has infiltrated the institutional church down through the centuries.

For example, Satan has been able to place unbelievers in positions of power within the church hierarchy. In the name of Christ and under these unbelievers, terrible crimes have been committed by religious institutions. These crimes have been committed against both those inside and those outside the church.

Still another overt accomplishment of Satan is the forming of countless bizarre groups. These groups claim to be Christian, even using Christ's holy name, and yet they do not believe Jesus Christ is God. Many of them even substitute their own so-called scriptures in place of God's Word, the Bible, but still call themselves "Christian."

Covert warfare. The Laodicean church, however, is a picture of Satan's *covert* strategy, built upon *deception.* Multitudes within the church are deceived into thinking the church is doing what is right and is pleasing God, when the opposite is true.

A large part of the institutional church today is very much the way Christ pictured the characteristics of the Laodicean church. This deception is possible today because the members of the "church" have very little personal knowledge of God's Word, the *objective* Authority of God's Truth. In addition to their lack of knowledge of the Bible, many church members have been taught that the "educated church leaders" are the "authorities" of God's Truth. It is time for us all to realize that God's Truth in the Bible is available to anyone who cares to study. God the Holy Spirit does communicate His Truth to us individually.

With increasing frequency, the "authorities" begin to make personal, *subjective* decisions about which parts of the Bible are infallible, which stories are mythological or allegorical, and which events of the Bible are "nonhistorical" or "nonscientific." As the Bible's *objective* authority is challenged, God's Absolutes and His Incredible Plan are less and less understood and believed. As members of the institutional church, you and I must constantly ask ourselves, "How did we allow this to occur?"

The means often used to soothe and satisfy the church attenders are the liturgy and the sacraments. Church attenders are taught the *supposed* progress in theological understanding while discussing the latest "myths" or "contradictions in the Bible." Christ is spoken of freely as the Son of God but there is a subtle subversion of Christ as the Infinite God who stepped into history: specifically He is referred to as "*the* Christ," the adopted son of God, a man especially chosen by God because of his perfect obedience. His death on the cross is viewed as a "noble example of sincerity of purpose" and merely the result of sinful men crucifying a good man. The children in Sunday school are taught complimentary words about Jesus but He is not presented as God, the One who came to die on the cross for their sins (*see* 2 Timothy 3:13–17).

Rather than faith in Christ as Saviour and Lord, the activity of the church focuses on the role it should play with its "good" works. Much *human* effort is expended upon these activities to "save the world." The rights of the people become the major concern rather than the righteous demands of a holy God. Relative values rule. Sin is viewed as making a mistake which a loving God would never hold against a person for eternity.

Many church members today evaluate their spiritual progress horizontally. That is, they evaluate themselves using comparative "human righteousness" or what might be called an assumption that "God grades on a curve" with "I've done the best I can" being entrance to heaven. Sadly, many church members are unwilling to face the stark reality of this widespread departure from biblical truth, and unable to understand the reason for the feeling of emptiness inside as they sit in church week after week. Today, you and I must recognize that even a slight deviation from God's Truth is the first step to complete apostasy. The loss of a personal relationship with God is quick to follow for the members of the church.

Another distortion of God's Truth is the current emphasis on an "experience" as the final criteria of spirituality. God can, and often does, give a believer an experience to validate His presence. To make experience the basis for Christianity rather than biblical content, however, is dangerous. Experience without content can lead to insidious deceptions since there is no objective truth to validate the source of a subjective experience.

In summary, Satan successfully uses a covert strategy to counterfeit the true church when the church members have neglected teaching God's Word.

The Missing Person. In the apostate church, the leaders administrate the church according to the world system while more and more becoming compatible with the values and methods of the world system. This is totally contrary to what Jesus taught, for He said that Satan runs the world system and that the Kosmos is incompatible with true Christianity.

The tragedy of the blending of the Kosmos (world system) and the church is that many people within the church do not have a personal relationship with the Person of Jesus Christ. Even though the church may have retained the name of Christ, it has largely lost the framework of God's Truth.

The members are often not aware that the Bible is one continuous story: God's story. They are not aware that the Bible is all true and totally relevant to each one of us. The predicament of much of today's church is the same as the Laodicean church: being well off and comfortable, feeling no need for a personal relationship with Christ. Christ is the Missing Person! Christ's evaluation of this kind of church is the same as it was of the Laodicean church: lukewarm, spiritually poor, and blind (*see* Revelation 3:15–19).

Christ's Solution.   Christ's solution for the apostate church is simple and direct: Return to Him. Every one of us needs Christ's Righteousness in order to approach God. Christ's loving invitation is described in Revelation 3:20 when the Bible states that Christ stands at the door of our hearts and knocks. If we are willing to open our hearts, Christ will come into our lives and we will have a personal relationship with Almighty God.

The Ultimate Trip

The hope of the church is called a mystery or a truth not previously revealed by God in the Old Testament. This mystery, or hope, is the wonderful moment when Christ comes for His church, that is, when Christ comes for all true believers. He told His disciples that He was going away to prepare a place for them but would return for them in person, in what will be the ultimate trip for believers (*see* John 14:1–3).

Paul relates three great acts of Christ's Omnipotence which will mark this hope called the translation of the church:

1. Christ will come with a shout which will resurrect all believing dead from their graves (*see* John 5:28, 29). They will be

transformed into beings with incorruptible bodies (*see* 1 Thessalonians 4:16; 1 Corinthians 15:52).

2. The living true believers will be transformed "in the twinkling of an eye" from mortal to immortal bodies (1 Corinthians 15:52, 53).

3. All true believers will be translated into the air to be with Christ their Lord. Literally, it means "to be seized away" or "caught up together" (1 Thessalonians 4:17).

This is the ultimate step in Christ's redemptive work: the changing of man's body from a weak, dying, "bound to earth by space and time" body to one like Christ's Resurrection Body (*see* 1 John 3:2). Paul states that in our present bodies we have a sense of waiting for their full redemption (*see* Romans 8:23). Not only will there be a change of body, but there will also be a change of position. Believers will be exalted with Christ, share His glory—and even reign with Him (*see* 1 Peter 5:6; Colossians 3:4; Revelation 3:21).

10

The Ultimate System:
Man's Kingdom Made "Perfect"

Just as history had a beginning on Planet Earth, it will also have an ending. This final time period, the ultimate world system, the cult of man, is described in the Bible, allowing us to know the history of a period yet to occur.

The importance of this final time period is evidenced by the amount of space given to it in God's Word. Twenty-five percent of Jesus' teachings were about His Second Coming and the events preceding it. The Old Testament prophets were given many specifics about this period. In addition, the entire Book of Revelation charts the sequence of these events which are to occur in the future.

Historical Note on the Beginning of the End

One of the most dramatic prophecies ever given is in the Book of Daniel. It presents a detailed timetable for the beginning of the end of the world system.

God's time clock started from the day a decree was issued allowing Jewish exiles to rebuild Jerusalem after their Babylonian captivity. The timetable runs until their Messiah was "cut off," or when He was crucified. This prophecy was revealed by the angel Gabriel who spoke to Daniel, saying, "Seventy weeks have been decreed upon your people and upon your holy city . . ." (*see* Daniel 9:24). It is necessary to understand that the Hebrew word translated as "weeks" is literally "sevens." Thus, the total period was to be seven times seventy, or 490 years.

From the restoration of Jerusalem to the death of Christ ("Messiah will be cut off") was 483 years. At some time in the future there will be a seven-year period ("week") which will end with the Second Coming of Jesus Christ.

The only event that needed to take place before this period of time was the establishment of the nation of Israel. For centuries,

people who studied prophecy in the Bible could not understand
how certain prophecies could be literal because they believed it to
be impossible that Israel would ever exist again as a sovereign
nation. This prophecy was literally fulfilled in 1948, however, and
the beginning of the Tribulation period is just waiting for the next
event that triggers the final days, the appearance of the Antichrist.

The Antichrist is the great personality who will head up this
world system, and he does so in the wake of a great "religious"
awakening. This awakening, however, will be the counterfeit
church which God calls the "great apostasy" (*see* 2 Thessalonians 2:3).

This world system and its "religion" will be so palatable and
tolerant that any "religious" view will be acceptable with one
exception. Significantly, this "religious" system will become the
bitter enemy of real believers who stand on God's Word and
believe in Christ as God: *they* will be persecuted and viewed as
intolerant bigots. The power of this religious system will be secret
and sinister, involving vast wealth. It is the fulfillment of Mystery
Babylon which we saw at Nimrod's time, and here God calls it
Mystery Babylon the Harlot (*see* Revelation 17:3–5). Since the
people on earth have maneuvered themselves into a position of
accepting a false messiah by rejecting the true Messiah, God will
send them the delusion of believing the lie. Actually, Antichrist *is*
the lie, the masterpiece of Satan (*see* 2 Thessalonians 2:11).

Antichrist

Antichrist gets his power by covenanting with Satan, the adversary of God, to sell his soul and freedom in return for ruling
power over the world. Christ refused to do this when He was
tempted by Satan, but finally Satan will find his man, one who will
truly be the "seed of the serpent" (*see* Genesis 3:15).

Antichrist gets his popularity and position by presenting himself as Christ and deceiving the world. This is the same pattern we
have observed from the beginning, in the mirror image of Figure
3. Not only does the Antichrist achieve popularity but he is actually able to convince people to worship him as god. This worship
comes to him by three different means:

1. His personal charm and charisma—coupled with supernatural ability and intelligence.
2. His superhuman power—displayed by signs and wonders.
3. His success—which is so supernatural that the majority will worship him.

Although the majority worships the Antichrist, he will compel the remainder of mankind to worship him also, under the penalty of death. He will use economic and military sanctions to prohibit people from buying or selling goods unless they bear the mark of Antichrist (*see* Revelation 13).

Many people wonder how the emergence of a world ruler such as the Antichrist could occur. We can see, however, that such a possibility is consistent with the period in which we are living. The breakdown of law and order, the growth of existentialist philosophy, and the prevalence of literature and films emphasizing the anti-hero or the absence of standards by which to make moral judgments, have destroyed the very foundation of existence in the world's civilization. This condition creates a void which demands to be filled. At the time when this meaninglessness and despair reaches an intolerable point, people will be receptive, or actually demand, that this void be filled. The public will eagerly seek someone or some force to bring order out of chaos, peace out of confusion, and love out of hate. This void will either be filled by God, who is able to fulfill all these needs, or by Satan, who will fill them with exact opposites that look like or mirror the real needs: counterfeit order, counterfeit peace, and counterfeit love. Virtually everyone will be deceived by the counterfeit when the world situation is sufficiently desperate. In today's world this counterfeit system could very easily rise to power by manipulation: convincing mankind that peace at any price is better than atomic war, that repressive order without individual freedom is safer than chaos, and that economic control is more desirable than runaway inflation. According to Francis A. Schaeffer, in his book *How Should We Then Live?* religion, even much of so-called Christianity, has little content and no base so people apathetically believe whatever is presented to them in a reasonable and "loving" way. This religious manipulation is the most dangerous because "as he thinks within himself, so he is" (Proverbs 23:7).

Worship of Antichrist.   The age-old ambition of Satan will finally be achieved when the majority of the world directs its worship toward the Antichrist, since Antichrist is the incarnation of Satan. This will occur in a worldwide system which is religious, economic, and political (*see* 2 Thessalonians 2:1–4).

   You might wonder why God would allow these events to occur. Since Eden, God has limited Himself to man's will permitting man to go his own way, building his own system. Throughout this time, God constantly loved man, sought him out, and revealed Truth to him. In the ultimate expression of love, God came in the Person of Christ to die for the sins of all mankind. For centuries, God has demonstrated incredible patience, giving humanity opportunity after opportunity to turn from their own system to God's Kingdom. Now, however, time is rapidly drawing to a close. In these final days, man worships Satan and willingly follows his leadership, and in doing so, clashes directly with Almighty God. The world system ends in chaos, anarchy, and death, the opposite of God's Kingdom.

The Tribulation

   The Tribulation is the biblical term used to describe the final days of the world system under the leadership of the Antichrist. This period of time is also called the Day of the Lord because it results in terrible but Just judgments by God on a world that continually follows Satan.

   When evil in man is not restrained and Satan has full sway, terrible chaos and destruction result. Just as at the Tower of Babel, fallen man without barriers accelerates the rate of rebellion greatly. Self-will, the original sin, results in lawlessness and anarchy (*see* 1 John 3:4).

Pseudopeace.   Pseudopeace will be forced by manipulation during the first half of the seven-year Tribulation. Antichrist will reign with power. During this three-and-a-half-year period, there will be a political, religious, and economic union which will be worldwide. Then suddenly, the "abomination of desolation" will occur in which Antichrist will attempt to deify himself. He will proclaim himself to be god and will establish himself in the Holy of Holies in the third Temple which will be located in Jerusalem (*see* Daniel 9:27; Matthew 24:15).

Great Persecutions. Great persecutions will occur during the last half of the seven-year Tribulation. The dictatorship of the Antichrist and the power of the world system will be directed against the Jews because they refuse to bow down and worship the Antichrist. During the Tribulation, the Jewish people, under the most adverse circumstances and persecution, will lead myriads and myriads of people to Jehovah God (*see* Revelation 7:9).

The message of the faithful of Israel will be the Good News that Jesus is the Messiah, He *is* their Lord. The Gospel of His Kingdom will be preached over the entire world (*see* Matthew 24:14).

Great Judgments. Persecution and judgment will dominate the last half of the Tribulation, leading to a great climax. Terrible persecutions will be carried out against the faithful of Israel and others who do not worship Satan, which in turn introduces the great judgments of God to be poured out on the world. The nations of the earth have been deceived and have worshiped Antichrist and now must be judged (*see* Revelation 13:11–18).

The judgments of the "great and terrible Day of the Lord" at first are simply the reaping of what man has sown. Man's rebellion results in chaos which leads to the dictatorship of the Antichrist. Then nature, which man has abused, will become barren as God acts against the earth, sea, rivers, and even the heavenly bodies which man in his rebelliousness has worshiped instead of God. Finally, Satan and his fallen angels will be allowed freedom on earth, bringing to a crescendo supernatural evil which even incorrigible sinners will not be able to tolerate.

God remains faithful to his Chosen People, the Jews, throughout these awesome events.

Armageddon

The greatest war of all time is about to begin, the logical result of man's rebellion. Rumors of invasion from the east and from the north will disturb the Antichrist and he will go forth with great anger to destroy and annihilate his enemies (*see* Daniel 11:44).

The battle plan involves coalitions and power struggles. "From out of the uttermost parts of the north . . . will come a mighty army against Israel like a cloud covering the land" (*see* Ezekiel 38:15, 16). Then from the Middle East, "Come, and let us wipe them out as a nation; that the name of Israel be remembered no more . . ." (Psalms 83:4). And finally from the east, ". . . the great river, the Euphrates, was dried up, that the way might be prepared for the kings of the east" (*see* Revelation 16:12).

The climax is Christ's return to earth and it is necessary for Him to return, literally, in order to keep mankind from obliteration (*see* Matthew 24:22). This is the great battle of Armageddon.

Christ's battle plan at Armageddon reveals His own attributes or *who He is*. His weapon of destruction is the Sword of the Word of God, coming forth from His mouth. It is with His **Word** that Christ will consume the Antichrist and destroy his armies.

It is the literal fulfillment of what Jesus reiterated over and over again while on earth the first time: that believing His Word results in Eternal Life but that not believing in Him would result in being judged by those very Words of His at the end of time (*see* John 12:48; Matthew 24:35).

11

The Ultimate Purpose:
God's Kingdom Made Perfect

As we move toward the conclusion of time, we discover that the end is really the beginning. These events, the culmination of history, are the last step of God's Incredible Plan.

Finally: Peace on Earth

Peace on troubled Planet Earth finally arrives when Christ returns, descending to the Mount of Olives, the exact spot from which He ascended (*see* Zechariah 14:4; Acts 1:9). At this time Jesus, who is the Prince of Peace, will reign from Jerusalem and all the believers from the Tribulation will enter this Millennial Kingdom. God's Chosen People, the Jews, will possess the land of Israel, fulfilling all the Old Testament promises. The church will also be with Christ as He reigns.

Jesus Christ will reign as King for a thousand years on Planet Earth (*see* Revelation 20:7). His reign will be characterized by peace and will include a well-ordered system of government. He will exercise Justice with Righteousness and all men on earth will have a complete and direct knowledge of God.

The Millennial Kingdom is the one which Adam forfeited and is sometimes called "Eden revisited." Christ, as the Last Adam, defeated Satan and regained the Kingdom by His work on the cross. In this thousand-year period, there will be healing of physical ills, restoration of long life, and no physical hazards. Great changes in the animal and vegetable worlds will eliminate violence among animals. "In that day the wolf and the lamb will lie down together, and the leopard and goats will be at peace. Calves and fat cattle will be safe among lions, and a little child shall lead them all" (Isaiah 11:6 LB). ". . . every knee shall bow . . . and every tongue shall confess that Jesus Christ is Lord . . ." (Philippians 2:10, 11 LB). Jesus is the Messiah who was prophesied hundreds of times throughout the Old Testament. During this time He reigns and will forever on the throne of David (*see* 1 Chronicles 17:14; Isaiah 9:7). He is pictured as both human and divine, being called the "Son of Man," "the Lord your God," and "the Mighty God."

Satan Bound. During the Millennial Kingdom, Satan will be bound in an "abyss" and thus will not be able to deceive the nations on Planet Earth (*see* Revelation 20:2, 3). This will enable people to see clearly that the hopes and goals of man can only be realized in the "kingdom of our God, and the Authority of His Christ . . ." (Revelation 12:10).

Prior to being bound, Satan promised world peace but delivered instead the destruction of worldwide war. He promised economic security but delivered economic ruin by controlling the world's money supply. He promised political unity and delivered a total dictator, Antichrist, whose forced worship of himself resulted in the worst bloodshed the world has ever known. But during the Millennium, Satan's power, which has plagued mankind since Eden, will be destroyed and removed from the earth. The real Kingdom of God will come to earth, ruled by the King of Peace and Love—Jesus Christ.

Trouble in the Kingdom. The Millennial Kingdom is a wonderful period populated by those persons who believed in Christ during the Tribulation. As wonderful as this Kingdom is, however, not all the descendents of the original believers will accept Christ as the Lord of their own lives. Man's sinful heart is still a problem.

This shows that even a perfect environment does not change a man's heart; only God can perform that miracle. Jesus said that *all* of us must be born anew spiritually through the work of the Holy Spirit. As we respond willingly to God's Love and accept His new Life, our sinful nature will be changed. The thousand years of the Millennium are God's proof to all created beings that environment and circumstances do not change a man's heart. Even complete knowledge about God does not bring everyone to Him to receive Eternal Life. Man's **Will** is the only deterrent and

God limits Himself to man's will. This is why Jesus defined His "family" as those who are willing to do the will of God. The quality necessary for eternity and for Eternal Life is **One Will— God's Will**.

The Final Rebellion.   Satan is loosed at the end of the Millennium and leads another, final rebellion against Christ. During the thousand-year period, there will be some who necessarily conform outwardly to the rule of Christ but who inwardly will be unbelieving. They will join Satan in this final attempt to destroy the perfect government with Christ as the Perfect Ruler. This illustrates dramatically the useless blindness and perversion of unbelief! At the same time God has proved His fairness and His right to judge.

Satan is finally placed in hell with all of his angelic followers (demons); thus carrying out God's judgment which He proclaimed at Satan's rebellion. At this time, also, all of unbelieving mankind is judged. They are judged according to their deeds because those persons chose to be judged by their deeds rather than to accept God's Provision for their imperfection. Every person who has ever lived has made the choice of accepting either God's will for his life or self-life apart from God. God's judgment of rebellious man is vindicated in that *it is man who chooses eternal separation from God.* "[God is] . . . not wishing for any to perish but for all to come to repentance" (2 Peter 3:9).

This is an awesome time in history when the rejected Love of God must become the Justice of God. Unbelieving man's deeds may be good or bad but they are from the tree of the knowledge of good and evil, which is death. No deeds are good enough for God to accept just as no deeds are evil enough that Christ's death is not adequate to pay for them. The issue has always been Eternal Life or eternal death, rather than good deeds or bad deeds.

New Heaven and a New Earth.   Jesus will vanquish every enemy, and the purpose of the Millennial Kingdom will then be fulfilled. At this time, every knee will bow in heaven and on earth and under the earth, and every tongue will confess that Jesus Christ is Lord (*see* Philippians 2:10, 11). Then Jesus will hand the

Kingdom over to God the Father (*see* 1 Corinthians 15:24). The heavens and earth will be consumed by fire and a New Heaven and a New Earth will be created (*see* 2 Peter 3:10–13; Revelation 21:1).

God's Will, Man's Will in One Accord

God's Incredible Plan has come full circle. This is what God has been working toward and eternity has begun. In Eternity Past God's will was challenged and time did not exist. At the point of rebellion against God's will, time began and the history of Planet Earth developed. We have seen how God solved the problem of man's rebellion with His Redemptive Plan, doing for us what we could never do for ourselves. Because of Christ's work on the cross all who willingly accept Him share in the riches of God's Grace forever. Eternity has begun.

Revelation 21 and 22 glowingly describe the vast riches of our future inheritance: the New Jerusalem. The apostle John in a vision from God ". . . saw the Holy City, the new Jerusalem, coming down from God out of heaven. It was a glorious sight. . ." (Revelation 21:2 LB). ". . . the home of God is now among men, and he will live with them and they will be his people . . ." (Revelation 21:3 LB).

All through the Bible the relationship between God and His people is compared to marriage. This is the bride of the Lamb (Jesus), the glorious Holy City called the New Jerusalem. The description before us is a community of believers who have placed their faith in Jesus Christ from all the ages, and the city in which they will dwell.

It is a most unusual city with only one street, one tree, and one river. Its size and shape are also amazing—". . . it was in the form of a cube, for its height was exactly the same as its other dimensions—1,500 miles each way" (Revelation 21:16 LB).

As John watched the New Jerusalem descend to the new earth "it shone with the glory of God" (*see* Revelation 21:11) and flashed and glowed like precious stones. This description beautifully pictures the perfection surrounding God. His glory is the radiant light illuminating the entire environment, and being reflected by the "precious stones": God's people.

We have difficulty grasping this perfection and glory in our present physical world with our imperfect relationships. Nevertheless, it is a real city and is very much a part of the "glorious hope" we have as believers! As our relationship with God deepens, this hope becomes even more exciting to us.

The river is called the Water of Life and is symbolic of the Eternal Life which everyone has in the New Jerusalem. Jesus repeatedly said while on earth that believing in Him resulted in a refreshing river of living water flowing from within. He was referring to the Holy Spirit living within a believer. (*See* John 7:37–39.)

The Tree of Life is the same tree which was in the garden of Eden, the Eternal Life of God. Again Jesus Christ taught His disciples that He is the Vine and we are the branches. "Take care to live in me and let me live in you. For a branch can't produce fruit when severed from the vine. Nor can you be fruitful apart from me" (John 15:4 LB). This Tree of Life in the New Jerusalem bears fruit each month, picturing Christ and the body of believers with the very life of Christ within them.

Even more significant is the fact that "no temple [structure] could be seen in the city, for the Lord God Almighty and the Lamb are worshiped in it everywhere" (Revelation 21:22 LB).

God's eternal purpose has always been to dwell with man. ". . . I will live in them and walk among them, and I will be their God and they shall be my people" (2 Corinthians 6:16 LB). (*See also* Exodus 29:45; Ezekiel 37:26, 27; Jeremiah 31:1.) This is called "tabernacling" and that is what Jesus did when He "became a man and dwelt [tabernacled] among us, and we beheld His glory . . ." (John 1:14). God's first house, the tabernacle in the wilderness, was rich in symbolism. (*See* Appendix B.) Christ fulfilled most of those types when He came to earth the first time as the "lamb of God," the "light," the "bread of life," and so forth. Now here before *us* is the fulfillment of the Holy of Holies.

The Holy of Holies was a perfect cube, 15' × 15' × 15' and that is where the Shekinah glory, the presence of God dwelt. The Holy City is a cube 1500 miles × 1500 miles × 1500 miles, the perfect fulfillment of that picture of God's dwelling place in the Old Testament tabernacle. The entire city is the Holy of Holies with the continual presence of God making it one spacious sanctuary.

Being people and limited as we are, we have such an inadequate understanding of the tabernacle (or temple) of God. The one description of this temple which we can understand, however, is that of believers being built up together into God's temple. "You are . . . fellow citizens with God's people and members of God's household . . . . the whole building is joined together and rises to become a holy temple in the Lord. And in him you too are being built together to become a dwelling in which God lives by his Spirit" (Ephesians 2:19–22 New International Version). This continual building program includes all believers in any age, who "as living stones are being built up as a spiritual house . . ." (1 Peter 2:5). Down through the ages, men and women have believed in God and become the materials being built up together into a constantly growing temple in which God dwells.

Abraham was one who looked forward by faith to this time when God's Incredible Plan would be completed. In Hebrews we read "Abraham trusted God, and when God told him to leave home and go far away to another land which he promised to give him, Abraham obeyed. Away he went, not even knowing where he was going . . . . Abraham did this because he was confidently waiting for God to bring him to that strong heavenly city whose designer and builder is God" (Hebrews 11:8, 10 LB).

Our Heavenly Father will have a family. As God's great workmanship, we become the fulfillment of His purpose. This unique corporate Body is growing up unto a Holy Temple. This is God's family. And here he is, man as he was created to be. He is in one accord with God, God's Will and his have become one, so also he is in one accord with his fellowman. The very things men have striven for so vehemently have been made a reality by God. Apart from God, man in his self-sufficiency can never bring into existence a world such as this.

As believers, we have a future life that is real, the new earth is a real place. It will exist and will be made of solid matter. We have an eternal life that is genuine, not ethereal; we will not float about in some ghostlike state. We will always have real bodies like Jesus' in the Resurrection, and we will be distinct individuals.

The new-ordered universe continues from this point forward in the realm of Eternity Future. The gifts of creativity and productivity given to man by God will be used in glory and honor, as visible evidence of the worth and value of mankind, and in perfect accord with God's will.

The physical condition of man in Eternity Future is that of complete health with no curse of pain or death. The resurrection body, also called the transformed body, will have complete affinity with the molecular universe and will be able to transverse it all (1 Corinthians 15). Man's emotional condition in Eternity Future is one of complete and unending happiness. Deep abiding joy will be pervasive, the result of hopes being realized.

God's Incredible Plan has come full circle. Will this earth change? *Yes.* Will the heavens change? *Yes.* Will the present Jerusalem change? *Yes.* Will we change? *Yes*—in the twinkling of an eye. God will dwell corporately and we will function as one with Him. We will live on Planet Earth forever in the perfect will of our Heavenly Father Who has loved us from the beginning.

12
Two Ways to God

At the end of any study of the Bible, Hal Lindsey suggests that we ask ourselves the question "So what?" He means "so what" does this mean to us personally? Just what difference does God and His plan make in our lives?

The two ways to God have sometimes been called Plan A and Plan B. Plan A is man's attempt to come to God by keeping the Law; Plan B is approaching God through grace—*His* gracious Provision for man's sin. This final chapter describes these two plans to God and the importance of choosing the correct one.

Plan A

To understand our dilemma, it is necessary to return to the beginning and consider again some basic truths. Simply stated, God created us to contain His Eternal Life and to mediate God's Kingdom on earth. Since Adam and Eve chose against God, their choice has also become our choice by inheritance. God told them what they must do but they chose against Him. To make it clear what He expected of people in order to come into His presence, God gave the *Law*.

The Law was given in three basic forms: the Law of God, the Law of Moses, and the Law of Christ. The Law of God refers to the law of moral consciousness written on man's heart (*see* Romans 1:19). By this basic Law of God, all people everywhere know of the existence of God and the need to live up to His moral Absolutes. The Law of Moses is an explicit, specific statement of God's Value System. This revelation of God's Value System was given to Moses in the Ten Commandments and in the civil and ceremonial laws entrusted to the nation of Israel.

The Law of Christ was given by Christ in the Sermon on the Mount (*see* Matthew 5–7). Through His teaching and in His Life, Christ both fulfilled the Law of Moses and revealed its full meaning. Christ made it clear that in God's viewpoint of the Law, the focus is upon the attitude of our heart and mind rather than only our outward physical actions as we attempt to keep the Law. As an example, Christ said, ''Under the laws of Moses the rule was, 'If you kill, you must die.' But I have added to that rule, and tell you that if you are only *angry,* even in your own home, you are in danger of judgment! . . .'' (Matthew 5:21, 22 LB). Christ continued, ''The laws of Moses said, 'You shall not commit adultery.' But I say: Anyone who even looks at a woman with lust in his eye has already committed adultery with her in his heart'' (Matthew 5:27 LB). After giving this very stringent definition of what keeping the Law involves, Christ made it clear that no violations are allowed when He stated, ''But you are to be perfect, even as your Father in heaven is perfect'' (Matthew 5:48 LB).

Human Responses to Plan A. How do you and I respond to Plan A as it has been revealed in its three forms? Everyone makes a response to these revelations of God's Law (*see* Romans 1–3), and an examination of people's behavior today and all through time reveals four typical response categories.

1. *Open rebellion against God.* One form of response is open rebellion against God. This is a response of unbelief. It is not really an intellectual problem of accepting that God is there. Rather, it is a moral problem. If a person admits that God *is* there and that the Bible is true, then that person's life is affected in substantial ways. He can no longer live as he pleases, denying God's Word and rejecting the concept of eternal judgment. If a person admits that God *is* there, he can no longer be his own god. Therefore, this person lives in rebellion against God in a vain attempt to deny God's reality.

2. *Human righteousness.* A second response to the Law is one of human righteousness. In this response, a person concentrates on being ''better'' than other people. Instead of focusing on God's standards of righteousness, this person compares himself or herself with others on a horizontal plane, using relative standards as goals for behavior. This person feels that he is not really ''too sinful'' and attempts to prove it through good deeds and social involvements, incorrectly reasoning that if he is ''doing the best he can,'' God will accept him on that basis.

3. *Legalism.* Another response to Plan A is found among those who believe they *can* keep God's Law. They base their approach

to God on *works* rather than faith. Since it is impossible to keep all of God's Laws completely, they select the "keepable" Laws, and then build traditions and doctrines on those "keepable" Laws. This leads to religious self-righteousness; such is the subtle egotism of man. The usual pattern is for persons who have developed such a legalistic pattern to extend it to exclusivism or a "keeping apart" from those who do not keep the Laws as they imagine they do.

4. *Repentance.* A fourth response—and the one God desires from each one of us—is one of turning to Him and trusting in Him. We finally acknowledge our inability to keep God's perfect Law, therefore recognizing what God intended from the beginning. To repent means to drop our rebellion against God, admitting the delusion of our human self-righteousness, and turn to God. We recognize our own sin and inability to meet God's requirement, and trust God to do what we cannot do for ourselves. Now we are candidates for Plan B, an approach to God on the basis of God's grace.

Plan B

Plan B is simple compared to Plan A. That may be one reason so many people have difficulty accepting it for their lives. In Plan B a person must recognize the fact that only God can provide for our righteousness and acceptability to Him. We cannot do it on our own. We must depend on God's grace.

God's grace is experienced by *faith*. Faith may be thought of as the believing attitude of our *will*. It is our response to God's ability. Faith is trusting God, who has proved over and over again, by His mighty acts through history, that He is trustworthy (*see* Acts 17:31).

God's Character.   God's character makes it necessary for us to approach Him under Plan B rather than Plan A. God is perfect and only perfect righteousness can be in God's presence. This places us in a terrible dilemma if we try to approach Him under Plan A. Our human righteousness—even among the "best" of humans—is pitifully inadequate compared to God's Perfect Righteousness.

The character of God is such that His Righteous judgment of

sin would result in death if taken by man himself. Instead, God has provided that His Righteous judgment be taken, not by man, but by man's Saviour. Christ's work on the cross provides the way—the only way—whereby God is *free* to love us and accept us into His own presence eternally.

Man's Condition Under Plan B.   The condition of man—all of us—is one of *im*perfection. To state it clearly, we are sinful. Through God's Provision (Plan B), all of man's sins have been placed, however, on the One Perfect Substitute—Jesus Christ. Our acceptance by God into His perfect Kingdom is based not on our own "good deeds," which are pitifully inadequate, but instead is based upon what Christ did on the cross, which is *infinitely* adequate. When we try to gain God's acceptance on our own merit, we are in effect saying that what Christ did on the cross is not good enough for us.

Our acceptance by God and its consequence of Eternal Life is a *gift of God's grace.* A gift, however, is not a gift unless it is accepted. We accept God's gift by believing in Jesus Christ and committing our will and our life to Him (*see* Ephesians 2:8, 9; 1 Peter 1:19–21; Titus 3:5).

Grace, Grace, and More Grace

To receive Eternal Life by grace is wonderful. Perhaps you have accepted His grace while reading this book or perhaps you have accepted it some time earlier. Thoughtful, serious consideration of God's attributes and His plan for our lives usually brings us to a realization that we cannot *earn* the right to live with God forever. It is logical and natural to accept, by faith, God's gift of grace.

We can accept God's grace for our Eternal Life but it is quite another thing to experience this same grace in our daily life as a Christian. Even as Christians, we are such practiced "legalists" with our dozens of rules! God has said *we are new creatures* in Christ (*see* 2 Corinthians 5:17), but our lifelong habits and our pride cause us to mix law and grace.

One reason we mix law and grace is that it is difficult to face up to the incorrigibility of our "old nature" which is "the body of sin" (*see* Romans 7). It is important, however, to see that if we put any confidence in our "old nature," we are living by the principle of the law. This will result in defeat in our walk with God and consequent guilt. Mixing law and grace in our new Christian life starts "civil war" within ourselves. To mix law and grace short-circuits the work of grace in our life.

Our daily walk with the Lord should be on exactly the same basis as our becoming a Christian: *by grace!* Walking continually by grace is also by faith and therefore effortless (*see* Colossians 2:6). Living by grace involves only faith—relying on the work of Another, the Holy Spirit, to make true in our life what God has already declared to be true, namely, that we are a new creature in Christ. In our new life, we will begin to experience love, joy, peace, patience, gentleness, kindness, goodness, and self-control (*see* Galatians 5:22, 23).

But mark this well: the effortless life is not the *will*-less life. Being "willing" simply means placing our faith in Christ and His ability rather than "trying harder" on our own.

It is not how much faith we have but rather learning how to focus the faith we have on Jesus as the only trustworthy Object. He is the One whose Power gave us our new life and whose same Power lives in us. The walk of faith consists of a believing attitude of our *will* toward Christ (*see* Romans 12:1, 2).

The progress in our walk as a believer comes not by effort on our part but by *growth,* and growth takes time. Our growth will naturally follow as we live each day understanding more and more that grace is God's *un*conditional, *un*limited Love. He not only accepted us initially when we responded to His grace but He also continually lives within us as our personal God—and He wants us to know Him personally in a growing relationship. This leads to the following very important summary statement about grace:

Understanding grace will result in feeling *comfortable* in God's presence so that we will turn to Him naturally and continually in every circumstance.

When we turn to God continually in every circumstance, we will get to know Him better and better.

Our Position in Christ. Experiencing God's grace daily is proportional to understanding our position in Christ. We may understand that our salvation was accomplished by grace but there is so much more to be experienced when we understand the total implications of our new position with God through Christ. This is more than just "salvation grace" and leads to the *application* of grace in our daily life.

Our position in Christ, as recipients of God's grace, includes many important facts. Some of the most important include the following. As believers we:

1. Have Eternal Life (*see* 1 John 5:11, 12).
2. Are in the Body of Christ, His church (*see* 1 Corinthians 12:13).
3. Are totally righteous (*see* 2 Corinthians 5:21).
4. Are totally forgiven (*see* Acts 10:34).
5. Have God's unlimited Power within us, through the Holy Spirit (*see* Acts 1:8).

These wonderful facts are true of us from the moment we receive Christ's Eternal Life and become new creatures. We can never get more of Christ than we receive the moment we believe. We can only grow in our understanding of our riches in Christ as we allow the Holy Spirit to conform us to His image (*see* Romans 8:29). Stated alternatively, the Christian life is *becoming* what we have already been made.

We make our greatest discovery when we understand that Planet Earth has a purpose and a plan—the Incredible Plan of the Eternal Creator. But our greatest joy comes when we discover that the same Eternal Creator also has a purpose and a plan for our personal lives. From the beginning, God loved us and desired that we respond and fellowship with Him. Through His gift of grace, He made possible the relationship we can have with Him in Christ. It is not *our* plan for being acceptable but rather God's plan which we accept by faith—letting Him live within us. So enjoy this great discovery and your own personal walk with Christ.

ALSO AVAILABLE

Two special packages are available to aid your understanding of *God's Incredible Plan.*

The PICTORIAL PANORAMA is a series of 10 full-color, 5" x 7" illustrations that will permit you actually to "see" *God's Incredible Plan* as it unfolds through the Bible. It is like viewing the "parade of life" from the perspective of eternity, or outside of time.

Also available is a STUDY GUIDE for individual study or group discussion. The guide outlines important concepts in *God's Incredible Plan,* keyed to the PICTORIAL PANORAMA. Each chapter contains additional helpful insights into God's plan as well as discussion questions and teaching suggestions for using *God's Incredible Plan* in classes and home-study groups.

ORDER PICTORIAL PANORAMA AND STUDY GUIDE BELOW

Please send

_____ copies of Pictorial Panorama (10 full-color, 5" x 7" illustrations of *God's Incredible Plan*) @ $2.95 each

_____ copies of STUDY GUIDE for *God's Incredible Plan* @ $2.95

COMBINATION SETS

_____ sets of PICTORIAL PANORAMA and STUDY GUIDE. Special combination price $4.95

ADD $.50 per order for postage and handling
Ohio residents add 4% sales tax

SEND ORDERS TO:

New Horizons Publishing
Box 3123
Columbus, Ohio 43210

APPENDIX A
The Existence of God Can
Be Logically Demonstrated

Since God's existence is an open question to contemporary minds, we feel it is of primary importance to present the reasons for believing in God.

Proving the Existence of God

Several basic approaches can be used to illustrate the existence of God. We have chosen three of them.

The *cosmological* argument is that the universe did not occur by chance. There must be a cause equal to its effect, and since the universe is likened to a clock which is running down (law of entropy; second law of thermodynamics), we must ask ourselves who wound up the clock and started it going? D. Elton Trueblood, in his book *Philosophy of Religion,* points out, "A clock which always runs down and is never rewound cannot have been running forever . . . . *Nature points beyond nature for an explanation of nature.*"

To believe the modern cosmological theory that the first cause was a "big bang," a cosmic explosion (what caused it is not known) about ten billion years ago, requires infinitely more faith from our viewpoint than to believe that God created the universe, and that He is the first Cause.

The *teleological* argument, which follows logically, has to do with the design in nature. When observing nature we are confronted with tremendous order and intricate design, all operating in predictable and repeatable patterns. Design points to a Creative Mind, a Master Designer who not only created all we see but who also has a purpose and a plan for His universe. As Paul the apostle said, "Since earliest times men have seen the earth and sky and all God made, and have known of his existence and great eternal power . . ." (Romans 1:20 LB).

To cite further evidence of intricate design let us consider the human eye. According to Garrett Hardin, quoted by Norman Macbeth in *Darwin Retried*, "If even the slightest thing is wrong—if the retina is missing, or the lens opaque, or the dimensions in error—the eye fails to form a recognizable image and is consequently useless." We do not believe such a complicated organ could have evolved in any step-by-step manner if, as evolutionists insist, each step involved a useful purpose of adaptation. A Master Designer is a far more likely explanation.

Further evidence of God's Creative Mind is the existence of only one genetic code for terrestrial life. If creatures sprang to life in some great "primeval soup" as evolutionists would have us believe, why are there not many different genetic codes? Multiple genetic codes would be much more consistent with chance and probability, which is the theory of those who reject God. The fact that there is only one genetic code is further proof of the Creative Intelligent Mind responsible for all life on Planet Earth.

What Is the Nature of the Designer?

The *moral* argument is that man has a built-in idea of right and wrong and of perfection. Although values change from one culture to the next, moral consciousness is universal. All men have it. Again, it is not possible to explain this idea of morality from the unconscious and inanimate universe, so we must look beyond and behind the universe. That is precisely what we do. We are as humans incurably "God conscious," and studies by anthropologists show that man has always had a basic built-in desire to know God and to understand His plan. When this basic desire has been distorted by idolatry and fear, man has developed very warped ideas in his religions but the "God consciousness" is still there.

C. S. Lewis, the great English philosopher, sums up this built-in morality in every person by saying that man does not call a line crooked unless he has some idea of a straight line. We believe God is that "straight line," the concept which He Himself placed within man.

God Is There

One of the greatest strengths of the Judaic-Christian faith is its rational and factual base. God is not only the Creator of the universe but He also personally communicates with us. His communication is in all areas of life; it is propositional Truth in written form, as well as objective, by acts in history. Paul the apostle points out that God furnishes proof to us by these acts which can be substantiated (*see* Acts 17:31). And so He validates Himself as a trustworthy Object of our faith, for it is true that any faith is only as valid as its object.

God Reveals Himself Here

Since we have chosen to believe that God is there it is natural to want to investigate the truth about Him. God reveals Himself here by various methods. We have discussed the universe and its design, as well as man's personality. Another even more specific way is His written Truth, the Bible.

The Bible is a direct, clear communication of God and His Incredible Plan to us in verbal form by using human authors to write down His unchanging Truth. God, in the Person of the Holy Spirit, insured the writing down of only God-breathed (which is another way of saying "inspired") Truth. This Truth is stated in this paraphrase of 2 Peter 1:21: "No prophecy [word from God] was ever made by an act of human will, but men moved by the Holy Spirit spoke from God." And further, "All Scripture is inspired by God . . ." (2 Timothy 3:16).

Since God has demonstrated His desire and ability to communicate to us we must also conclude that the Bible is a perfect communication, understandable and preserved down through time without error. Spanning over a thousand years, its sixty-six books have incredible unity and a progression of revealed truth about God and man. In addition, the Bible has the merit of being substantiated historically, prophetically, and morally by men of all eras.

APPENDIX B
The Tabernacle

The command was first given to the children of Israel, "And let them construct a sanctuary for Me, that I may dwell among them" (Exodus 25:8).

The dwelling or Tabernacle was a tent, because the people among whom God came to reside were wandering and had not yet reached their Promised Land. Later this tent was replaced by Solomon's Temple, and still later by the rebuilt Temple after the Babylonian captivity. Today the Temple is the Body of Christ (the church universal), the dwelling place for God. The true believers who contain the Eternal Life of Christ make up "the Temple of the living God."

Christ's finished work on the cross is so clearly seen as we look back through time: first the altar, then the Tabernacle, later the Temple, and now the Body of Christ (the church).

The Pattern of the Tabernacle

God was the Architect of the tent which He called "the pattern of things in heaven" (*see* Exodus 25:9). (The reader should refer to the floor plan of the Tabernacle which precedes this chapter.)

Entering the court from the outside, the last object to be reached was the Holy of Holies, into the very Presence of God.

The Court and the Gate (*see* Exodus 27:9–17). We begin on the outside where every person must begin who would see the Kingdom of God.

The white linen fence completely hid the Tabernacle, for it was eight and a half feet high. There was one gate or door on the east end, a picture of what Christ said of Himself: "I am the door; if anyone enters through Me, he shall be saved . . ." (John 10:9).

The Brazen Altar (*see* Exodus 27:1–8).   He who entered the gate came first to the altar. ". . . without the shedding of blood there is no forgiveness of sins" (Hebrews 9:22 LB). Right inside was the altar, which was four feet square and was called the brazen altar, for it was made of wood covered with brass. Altars had been used from the beginning for sacrifices to be offered to God. The sacrifice pictured the fact that sin must be punished by death and God's principle of an innocent life substituted for the person who had sinned.

The worshiper brought an animal to the altar. The priest tied the animal fast to one of the horns on the corner, placed his hand on the head of the animal, and prayed. He was confessing his sins and the sins of the person who brought the sacrifice, asking God to accept the death of the animal in place of the death of the sinner.

Christ is our substitute today, and His "altar" was the cross. ". . . He humbled himself by becoming obedient to the point of death, even death on a cross" (Philippians 2:8).

The Laver (*see* Exodus 30:17–21).   The laver which stood at the entrance to the tent contained water and was for washing. Only the priest could go beyond this point into the tent, for it meant death to enter the Holy Place without first washing at the laver. Today the cleansing by Christ Himself washes us clean so that we can enter God's presence.

The Candlestick (*see* Exodus 37:17–24).   What was it like inside the curtain? Only the priests could enter this first room of the Tabernacle called the Holy Place. There were no windows and the only light was from the candlestick which stood along the south wall. It was made of solid gold and the light from the burning oil was never allowed to go out. Jesus Christ claimed to be the Light of the world fulfilling the image presented by the candlestick (*see* John 8:12).

The Table of Shewbread (*see* Exodus 25:23–30).   On the north wall, opposite the candlestick, was the table of shewbread which was made of wood covered with gold. Every Sabbath there were twelve loaves of bread placed on the table which stood for the twelve tribes of Israel and looked forward to Christ who said, "I am the bread of life; he who comes to me shall not hunger . . ." (John 6:35).

The Altar of Incense (*see* Exodus 30:1–5). The third piece of furniture in the Holy Place was the altar of incense. It was small, only eighteen inches square and three feet high. Sweet-smelling incense was burned day and night. In the Bible, prayer and worship are spoken of as incense. Just as the incense burned continually in the Holy Place, Jesus Christ prays continually for us. ". . . He always lives to make intercession for them" (Hebrews 7:25).

The Holy of Holies (*see* Exodus 25:10–22; 37:1–9). "And there I will meet with you . . ." (Exodus 25:22). "Let us therefore draw near with confidence to the throne of grace, that we may receive mercy, and may find grace to help in time of need" (Hebrews 4:16).

The Veil. The veil at the door of the Holy Place invited the priests to draw near, but the veil separating the Holy Place from the Holy of Holies forbade entrance (*see* Exodus 26:33). "Cherubim of glory" (Hebrews 9:5) were embroidered on the veil guarding the entrance to the Holy Presence of God.

While the veil was intact, the way into the Holy of Holies (the Presence of God) was closed (*see* Hebrews 9:8). It was awaiting the death of Christ. When Christ died on the cross this veil was torn from the top to bottom (by the hand of God), opening the way into the very Presence of the Holy God (*see* Matthew 27:51).

The Ark (*see* Exodus 25:10–22; 37:1–9). At first glance the ark appeared to be one piece of furniture. However, if one looked closely it would become apparent it was composed of two parts. The lower portion was called the ark of the covenant. It was a wooden box overlaid with gold. Its dimensions were about four feet long, two feet wide, and two feet high. The top was called the mercy seat and was made of solid gold. It was actually the lid of the box. At either end of the mercy seat was a cherubim made of solid gold. God had said to Moses, "I will meet with you from above the mercy seat, from between the two cherubim" (*see* Exodus 25:22).

Inside the ark were the tablets of stone on which the Ten Commandments were written, the gold container of manna, and Aaron's rod.

Once a year on the Day of Atonement (the most solemn day of the year), the high priest met with God in the Holy of Holies on behalf of the people of Israel. He caught the blood of the sacrificial animal in a basin, carried it into the Holy of Holies, and sprinkled it on the mercy seat. When the high priest came out the people knew that God had accepted their offering and they were forgiven.

As the high priest entered into the Presence of God with the blood of the animal offered for the sins of the people, so Christ entered into the Presence of God with, not the blood of animals, but His own blood. It was a never-to-be-repeated offering. "And every priest stands daily ministering and offering . . . sacrifices, which can never take away sins; But He [Jesus Christ], having offered *one* sacrifice for sins *for all time*, sat down at the right hand of God" (Hebrews 10:11, 12, author's italics).

The Objective of the Tabernacle

The immediate objective of the Tabernacle was to bring God near to the Israelites, to reveal His Holiness, and to have fellowship with them.

At that point in God's Incredible Plan, the Israelites would certainly, without such visible help, have gone away from Him. Until God came in the flesh in the Person of Jesus Christ, even the most devout believers sought to lay hold of some visible link of communion. Had they been able to see from our point in time, they would have been lifted above the necessity of earthly types and shadows of eternal truths.

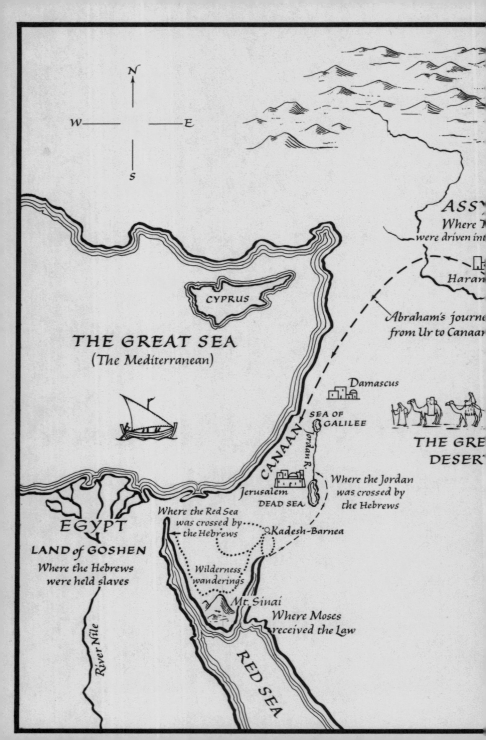